THE FORGOTTEN TRIBES, ORAL TALES OF THE TENINOS AND ADJACENT MID-COLUMBIA RIVER INDIAN NATIONS

by

Donald M. Hines

Great Eagle Publishing, Inc.
Issaquah, Washington

THE FORGOTTEN TRIBES, ORAL TALES OF THE TENINOS AND ADJACENT MID-COLUMBIA RIVER INDIAN NATIONS

By Donald M. Hines

published by:

Great Eagle Publishing Inc.
3020 Issaquah-Pine Lake. Rd. SE
Suite 481
Issaquah, WA 98027 — 7255
U.S.A.

First Printing 1991

PUBLISHER'S CATALOGING IN PUBLICATION
(Prepared by Quality Books)

Hines, Donald Merrill, 1931-
The forgotten tribes, oral tales of the Tenino and adjacent Mid-Columbia River Indian nations / by Donald Hines — p.cm...
Includes bibliography \ ISBN 0-9629539-0-3
1. Tenino Indians — Legends. 2. Watlala Indians — Legends.
3. Umatilla Indians — Legends. 4. Indians of North America — Legends. I Title
E98.F6 979.500497 MARC

CONTENTS

PART ONE
INTRODUCTION

PART TWO
THE TENINO OR WARM SPRINGS INDIANS

PART THREE
THE UMATILLA INDIANS

PART FOUR
THE *WATLALA* OR CASCADES INDIANS

ILLUSTRATIONS

PLATE 1: Surrounded by sere desert, the mouth of the Deschutes River as seen from the Washington

side of the Columbia River. (Interstate 84 traverses the southerly river bank.)

PLATE 2: A Umatilla mat lodge. Edw. S. Curtis photo, c. 1910.

PART ONE

INTRODUCTION

THE SETTING, PROVENANCE, AND ORGANIZATION OF THE TALES OF THE TENINOS AND NEARBY MID-COLUMBIA RIVER INDIAN NATIONS

A. Geographic Locale

The territory of the Indian tribes of this volume extends westward along the Columbia River from the modern town of Umatilla, Oregon, and the Umatilla River where it flows into the Columbia. The Umatilla river's mouth is broad and quiet now, but in times past was a likely salmon spawning site and, therefore, an Indian fishery and village site. About 60 miles to the west the Deschutes River enters the Columbia River. Similar to the Umatilla River, the Deschutes is a broad and shallow stream, another likely salmon spawning site and Indian fishery, also village-site of some Tenino Indians. But extending westward from below Hood River, Oregon, to the mouth of the Willamette River, at Portland, Oregon, was the general territory of the Watlala or Cascades Indians. The name "Cascades" refers to the lower system of rapids of the Columbia

River (now flooded behind Bonneville Dam), along which the Indians dwelt and fished.

The Eastern Oregon locale of the Umatillas and the Teninos consists of a desert-like plateau region of treeless basaltic wastes covered with thin soils which receive scant rainfall per year. The region's winters are often very cold indeed, and summer temperatures can exceed 100° F.. On the easterly slopes of the Cascades Range, or else the Blue Mountains, game such as deer was hunted. But the teeming spring and summer migrations of salmon undoubtedly occupied all these tribes in fishing, and in drying salmon against the winter. Below Hood River, Oregon, the landforms change: over time the Columbia River has cut a deep gorge and rapids-choked channel through the Cascades Mountains, nearby Mount Hood towers at 11,245 ft. The Cascades mountain slopes are heavily forested in virgin stands of Douglas fir and other connifers. The westerly slopes of the mountains receive very much rain from the warm, moist currents of air brought with the Japanese current, and the Pacific Ocean, while in winter the mountains receive an extensive snow pack.

But the dominant geographic feature of the area is the Columbia River, one of America's great rivers. Before 1957 and the closure of The Dalles Dam, from modern Wishram, Washington, (across from the mouth of the Deschutes River) to near modern Bonneville, Oregon, the Columbia River was a raging, deadly series of two systems of rapids, or "dalles." The great upper rapids extended from Wishram westward to near the city of The Dalles, Oregon. The Cascades, or lower rapids extended from just below the town of Hood River, Oregon, westward to near Bonneville,

Oregon. The systems of rapids made the river essentially unnavigable, that the Indians simply portaged about them. The unwary river traveler, who failed to turn aside in time from before the rapids, was doomed.

B. The Indians and Their Cultures

The great distances from the tribal area of the Umatillas, westward to the Teninos, still further westward to the area of the Cascades or Watlala Indians likely boasted of other Indian tribes as well. But only one of this area's tribes has had their traditional culture collected and studied in detail — the Wishrams who lived opposite The Dalles, Oregon; the oral traditional literatures have been collected in some depth for but two tribes: the Wascos and the Wishrams. Alas, the time is past, and the life and lore of tribes now vanished is beyond recall. Thus, the tales here are extraordinarily important: there are none others extant.

In the preparation of this volume, we have tried *first* to present a useable if terse sketch of cultural life against which the traditional tales might have real dimension. But we are so far disappointed, for scientific descriptions far back enough in time to be authentic, detailed and objective are hardly available. And what is extant is noted in the "Selected Bibliography" at the back of this volume. Accordingly, we have attempted to visit and physically to explore the locale of at least two of the tribes, to walk the vicinity, in order to undergird the inferences which we must make in the brief sketches before each tribe's tales.

The tales in the collection were originally labeled with names which may have been used by the tribes themselves, or else were in popular parlance. The first group of tales are from the "Warm Springs Indians." But we have assigned another, hopefully more accurate name to these tribespeople: *Tenino.* And for these reasons:

a. No such Indian *tribe* as the "Warm Springs" exists — only a reservation.

b. Indeed, the "Warm Springs Reservation" was peopled by elements of Wasco, Paiute, Tyigh, and Tenino.[1] *Tenino* was a general tribal name for the Indians who dwelt at or near the junction of the Deschutes River with the Columbia River. But about fifty miles south of its estuary, the Deschutes River now forms the easterly boundary of the Warm Springs Confederated Indian Reservation.

c. The "Warm Springs" Indians were likely river dwellers originally, and most likely dwelt far enough up the Columbia River as to be within traveling distance that some of them might have talked with or worked for L. V. McWhorter (the collector of this lore) in the vicinity of the Yakima Confederated Indian Reservation.

d. The first raconteur of a "Warmsprings" tale was *Lu-pa-hin*, also known as Caesar Williams. A permanent resident of the Yakima Reservation, married to a Yakima, he was an ". . . hereditary chief of the Warm Springs tribe. . . ." In fact, he was perhaps a Tenino.

e. The setting of the tale narrated by *Lu-pa-hin* is placed about the Columbia River close by the modern town of Wishram, Washington, where the great upper rapids began on the Columbia. Wishram is opposite the mouth of the Deschutes River. The other tales' settings are indeterminate.

f. In walking 3-5 miles southward from the Columbia along the banks of the Deschutes River (now the site of an Oregon state park, the banks well trod by eager, modern fisherfolk), the site seemed a likely setting for fishtaking, also to sustain and to support village life. At this point the river is quite broad, and shallow, an opportune fishing site at which to net or to trap great numbers of spawning salmon.

   The ethnographic studies done by George P. Murdock of Tenino Indians whom he visited on the Warm Springs Reservation, provides an extraordinarily useful means by which to perceive everyday tribal life as it must have been. We have taken the opportunity to note the parallels of culture form and function of the Tenino with their cross-river neighbors, the Wishram.[2]

Second, the "Umatilla" Indian tales have proven no less difficult to establish a culture base for. And for these reasons:

a. Landform names provide some help in locating the tribal locale, in that a river, a town, even the county all bear the name: Umatilla.

b. The narrative settings include some further help, for one of the tales specifies: "around Walla Walla," or "in the Umatilla country;" another: hunting in the "Blue Mountains."

c. But an authentic, detailed cultural description or study is not apparently available, and we have presumed again to walk along the mouth of the Umatilla River so as to inform our inferences. As it enters the Columbia, the Umatilla Rivver takes on a similar character as the Deschutes River: considerable breadth, shallow depths, an appropriate site for salmon spawning, but also an opportune place especially for salmon netting, etc. Again the river locale promises a source of food, of water, and the sheltering confines of a gently sloping basin about the river within whose thin, tree-fringed banks an Indian village might have been placed.

Third, the "Cascades" Indians refer to a tribe(s) dwelling westward from the Klickitats, and perhaps on both sides of the Columbia River, from below Hood River to Portland, Oregon and the mouth of the Willamette River. This tribe bears the name *Watlala.*[3] Most likely decimated by pestilances during the early 19th century, the Watlala were absorbed by other tribal entities, or else have disappeared. To provide a cultural context is most difficult; cultural data for the Watlala Indians is quite lacking. But we assign the narratives as Watlala for these reasons:

a. The source of almost all the "Cascades" narratives is the very excellent tale-teller in his own right, Owl Child. Reared as a Wishram and with familial ties to the Wascos, he terms the tales which he tells as "Cascades," as of that tribe. If little study has been made of the secondary raconteur and his expertise, we opt to accept Owl Child's description as likely.

b. Still another informant, Chief Meninock describes the version which he tells as an "*n-Chewana*" legend — this informant was reared along the Columbia River at Skein,[4] and so likely was acquainted with the body of tales which he had heard as a youth from some of the Watlalas.

c. Still another detail in tale 10A, reputedly told by the Watlala, names a specific Cascades Indian personality.

d. The Watlala likely fished the lower rapids of the Columbia River, and accordingly dwelt at or near productive fishing sites or salmon spawning rivers such as the Sandy River, the Washougal River.

C. Intent of this Work

This work presents some exemplary tales from the oral traditions of the Teninos, Umatillas, and Cascades or *Watlala* Indian nations. These tales have not been rewritten, nor are they modern "remembrances of convenience." Instead, these texts are traditional:

they were told by Indians who had learned them as youths from tellings by tribal elders, who treasured them for their unique structure and subject. The tales are also authentic: they were taken down from Indians who still commanded their tribal language and lore. They were not taken up from some book, not contrived or composed at this late date. Indeed, the tales come from far enough back in the past, that it was possible to discover tribal memories in full possession of original unique tribal lore. But that time has past in the 50-70 years since these narratives were taken down. No longer does tribal memory strongly sustain the past. But these tales are presented with the hope that still other collections of tales, long since written down and put by, may yet be discovered.

These narratives were collected a short while after Lucullus V. McWhorter moved to the vicinity of the Yakima Indian Reservation in 1903 to take up ranching. His prior interests in archaeology, of Indian culture and life, and especially traditional lore, were aroused in his new locale.

For four decades until his death in 1944 McWhorter continued to collect and to preserve a record of traditional Indian culture found on or by the Yakima Indian Reservation, culture which he perceived was already fading from tribal memories. At his death in 1944, his papers were placed in the library-archives of Washington State University, Pullman, Washington. Included are thousands upon thousands of items: books, photographs, manuscripts, journals, manuscript fragments, letters, and mementos.

Of particular interest is McWhorter's effort to collect the oral myths, legends, tales and other narratives of the Yakima, Klikitat, Wasco and Wishram, and other tribal groups. Self-taught, McWhorter patterned his collecting methods after the bare outlines of collecting particulars obtained from the Bureau of American Ethnology, details found subsequently in his papers. Commonly he collected narratives heard around a campfire, after a hunt, or narratives recited during a longhouse ceremony — in proper context. McWhorter would listen, and then as soon after as possible would write or typewrite from memory the narratives which he had heard. Or, his Indian friends wrote down and translated into English for him numerous tribal narratives. Having considerable facility with the Yakima language, McWhorter sought to be accurate, detailed and thorough. He did not rewrite tales into literary forms like the short story. Instead, he often appended his questions and an informant's answers which explained numerous details of the stories, or he cited useful cross-references. What is of critical importance — McWhorter collected and added to his files all sorts of Yakima and other tribal narratives — from a myth to a legend to a magical belief — ***and more***. No practiced folklorist, he knew little of the conventional genres and when to stop collecting; so he collected all that he heard. And he collected in depth as best he know how — his labors are a priceless legacy of traditional oral life and lore from the region's Indian nations.

This work, then, sets forth authentic versions of told Indian tales and legends for the Tenino, Umatilla and Watlala Indians. The narratives were originally taken from and translated from Indian sources. They have not been rewritten after bookish literary forms.

Bibliographic annotation from without the immediate Mid-Columbia River area only emphasizes the traditionality of the tales: as deriving from an oral milieu, conforming to tradition; as vital narrative forms, an inimical part of tribal culture.

The texts, as collected by L.V. McWhorter, were extracted from Folders 1511, 1512, 1513, 1515, 1516, 1522, and 1523 of the McWhorter Papers, Washington State University Library, as cited in Nelson A. Ault 1959. *The papers of Lucullus Virgil McWhorter*. Pullman: Friends of the Library, State College of Washington, pp. 101-106. These narratives have not appeared previously in print.

And with the kind permission of Dr. Earle Connette and his staff, and his successor, Mr. John Guido, I turned over the fading, penciled pages of this collection. Using photocopies of McWhorter's original texts supplied me by the WSU library staff, I have made only those minimal changes of spelling or direct discourse to maximize reader understanding. The tales have not been rewritten, but preserve the oral sense of their original narration.

Our study and presentation of the traditional tales here is most deliberate. In creating this work we have especially relied on Laurits Bødker 1965. *Folk literature (Germanic), international dictionary of regional european ethnology and folklore*, Vol. II, ed. Ake Hultkrantz. Copenhagen: Rosenkilde and Bagger. And we have freely consulted Stith Thompson 1946. *The folktale*. New York; relied greatly on his *Tales of the North American Indians* (Bloomington, Ind., 1966), and other works.

D. Organization of the Work

The traditional narratives in this volume have been grouped into tribal categories. Within each category, the tales bear a descriptive title, given by the Indian raconteur or by another. Then, each narrative is given a number which marks its place within the volume, along with variants or comparable versions. More, details describing the informant from whom the tale was taken down and the time of the original narration plus other details about the tale are given. Especially have McWhorter's original notes been retained.

To assist the reader, several informational features are appended hereafter. First, an *Index of Motifs* contains traditional details of character, plot, or other background detail in the narratives. Second, *Comparative Notes* cite similar narratives from other Plateau Indian tribes. Third, a *List of Informants* contains biographical detail, if available, about each tribal taleteller . Fourth, *Notes to the Narratives* provide explanatory details about the narratives, and were taken from informants to McWhorter or to Murdock. To assist the inquiring student, a *Selected Bibliography* of useful works on the tribal life and lore of the Teninos, Umatillas, et al., is included. Finally, *Acknowledgements* of sources and individuals to whom we are indebted concludes this work.

PLATE 3: The Deschutes River, looking upstream, southward. A blue heron feeding in the photo's upper right attests to the stream's shallowness.

Photo by author.

PART TWO

THE TENINO-WARM SPRINGS INDIANS

I. THE TRADITIONAL NARRATIVES

1. *NASH-LAH*
Lu-pah'-kin, 1913

Chief Coyote had five sisters, and he carried them in his stomach.[5] They were the Huckleberries and were wise. When he wanted to know about anything, he went to them. They knew everything, and Coyote often held council with them. So when Coyote heard that someone was killing the people as they traveled up and down the *n-Che-wana*, he said, "I will stop it! I will stop this killing of the people."

Coyote called on his five sisters to tell him what to do. They said, "We will not tell you this time. When we tell you anything, you always say, 'Yes! I knew that. I knew it already.'"

Coyote got mad. He said to his sisters, "Unless you tell me, I will call the rain. You will get wet."

Rain would kill the sisters, destroy them. They became scared! They said, "No! Do not make it rain. We will tell you all about it. We will tell you what to do. Get plenty of dry wood and pitch. Carry five sharp flint knives with you. It is *Nash-lah*[6] at Wishom who is killing all the people. He is swallowing them as they pass up and down the *n-Che-wana* in canoes."

Coyote said to the sisters, "Yes! That is what I thought. I knew it already."

Nash-lah lived in the *n-Che-wana* where the water was deep. He would not let the canoes pass. He[7] swallowed all the people who came that way. But when he saw Coyote, he knew him to be the Great Chief. *Nash-lah* would not swallow Coyote. Coyote taunted him, called him all kinds of bad names. *Nash-lah* grew mad and drew Coyote in with his breath. As he went, Coyote grabbed a big armful of sagebrush and took it with him. When he arrived inside of *Nash-lah*, he found many of his people, Animal People. They were cold and hungry. Coyote said to them, "*Ow-eih* [Salutation]! You all here, too? Well, my people, I will build a fire in this place so you can come and warm, so you can come and eat."

The people had never had a fire in there, had nothing to eat. It was a long time that they had been starving. Many of them were nearly dead. Coyote made a good fire. He told the people to come close and get warm while he fixed something for them to eat. He said, "I am going to kill *Nash-lah*. That is why I am here, my people. I have come to help you, help you to live. You will not die."

Coyote built the fire under the heart of *Nash-lah*. He took one of his flint knives and began to cut the heart out of *Nash-lah*. He cut pieces to roast for the starving people. He worked while the people got warm and ate. He used all but one of his arrowhead knives, wore them out or broke them. Coyote took the last of his knives, the fifth knife. With it he cut the last of the great heart. It fell to the floor, which killed *Nash-lah*. As he died, he gave one great cough and threw the people all out on the shore of the *n-Che-wana*. When all were on land, Coyote called them together and said, "I told you I would save you. It is my work; I have done so. You did not die. You are alive and will live."

Coyote then gave all the people names. Eagle was to be the bravest and best bird. Owl was to be a big medicine man. Wolf was to be the best hunter; Bear was to be the strongest. *Qee-nut* [Salmon] was to be the best of all fish, the best salmon. Sturgeon was to be the largest in the rivers. Coyote named Beaver, Lynx, Fisher, *Wahk-puch* [Rattlesnake] and all the other animals and birds. He called himself Coyote, the wisest, the smartest of all animals. He said to *Nash-lah*, "You will have to quit killing the people as you have been doing. A new people [Indians] are coming, and they have to live. They will pass up and down the *n-Che-wana*. You cannot be so great and kill them all. You may occasionally kill just a few, but you cannot be the big man as you have been. You can shake the canoes if they pass over you, and maybe draw them under the water. For this reason the canoes will mostly go around you and not pass over where you stay. This is to be the law always."

That law stands, and to this day *Nash-lah* has not swallowed the people as of old. He has not swallowed them as he did before Coyote killed him and took away his big power. He lives deep under the water, where he always lived, but he is no longer so powerful. Sometimes he draws a canoe under and drowns the Indians in it, but not often. They go around where he lives, do not pass over his home.

The first steamboat that the whites brought up the *n-Che-wana* was stalled by *Nash-lah.* The Indians told the whites to throw food into the river, and then they could go. They did so, threw overboard sugar, flour, rice and other things. *Nash-lah* then let the boat loose.

2. THE *PAH-HO-HO KLAH*
Ah-nah-chu Pick-wah-pah ("Behind the Rock")

Hunting in Oregon, I got lost in fog and rain. I killed one deer. I carried that deer. I did not get crazy! I did not run like wild. I thought to stay where I was when the fog came up, wait till all cleared away again. I do this when I find I am lost. It is not good to travel when lost. You might get killed. There are high rocks where you fall and die. I got under a big tree, a heavy-topped tree. With plenty of dry wood, I built a fire out from the tree; I took a place between the fire and tree. I was close against tree, a safe place. I roasted meat from the deer and ate.

Not long after this I heard calling, calling like birds in the trees about my camp. It was getting dark! Other voices like birds answered farther away. I knew the birds were not there.[8] It was the *Pah-ho-ho Klah*[9], the little people of the mountains. I was scared! I did not answer them! I sat still! I did not move, did not make any noise. If I answered the calls, I would go crazy, be lost five days and five nights. It would rain and be foggy five days and five nights. I sat against the tree in the firelight, holding my gun. I watched just like a soldier! I did not sleep all day. I kept the fire burning, watching everywhere. The sun traveled behind the clouds; no light was in the woods.

Night came, dark, still plenty of fog, wet rain. I must sleep! I made a big fire to light up all around the camp. I lay down, my feet to the fire and my head close against the tree. I slept long. I did not know how long I slept; then I awoke. There! I looked good! I looked sharp! Only a short distance from me, in the light of the fire, I saw him! I saw the *Pah-ho-ho Klah*! He was sitting down, had an arrow! Yes! He was biting that arrow, sighting it with his eye! Yes! He was making the arrow straight.

I looked at him fixing his arrow. I saw him good. He had on buckskin clothes, a shirt filled with holes, a summer-shirt. I can make that shirt. He had a band of cedar bark this wide [two fingers] tied around his head. His hair was braided like mine, hung to the middle of his breast, maybe a little shorter. I saw above his left shoulder the feather-ends of about ten arrows and a bow, all in a case on his back. The *Pah-ho-ho Klah* was Indian all right, the same color as me. He was straightening arrows with his teeth, biting out crooked places. I was not scared now. I lay still. I was lots sleepy. I went to sleep again.

The next morning it was getting light; I heard the same voices! They went farther, farther away! After calling five times out in the woods, then they quit. The *Pah-ho-ho Klah* Chief had called his people from that place. The rain had now quit; the fog was thin, waving like wind. The sun came up, shining warm. I went up on a hill, looked everywhere. I knew that country; I knew where I was. I carried the deer, traveled to camp about three hours. I was safe! I am telling you this tonight.[10]

3. BATTLE BETWEEN EAGLE AND OWL

Eagle was a great hunter, and Owl a great medicine man. A dispute arose between them as to their powers in battle. They fought! They flew upward as is Eagle's wont, but Owl kept with him, plucking out his feathers. Out of sight they went, and finally Owl succeeded in tearing out the last feather of Eagle. This last feather was the central or bearing-up feather of his tail. Eagle, who always killed so many people of the air, fell lifeless to the ground. Owl, whose medicine was the strongest, returned victor to the earth.[11]

PLATE 4: The middle Columbia River. Edw. S. Curtis, photo, c. 1910.

PLATE 5: An old man of the *Wai-Yam,* Indians who dwelt near Celilo Falls. Edw. S. Curtis photo, c. 1910.

II. "THE TENINO INDIANS"[12,13]

The Tenino, also called the Warm Springs Sahaptin, at their first contact with Europeans occupied a portion of the south bank of the Columbia River in north central Oregon and the lower watershed of its southern affluents.[14] Their immediate neighbors, reading clockwise, were the following tribes: the Sahaptin-speaking Umatilla to the east beyond ca. 120°5' W; the Shoshonean-speaking Northern Paiute to the south beyond ca. 44°55' N; the Waiilatpuan-speaking Molala across the Cascade Range (ca. 121°45' W) to the west, whence they had been driven by the Tenino in late protohistoric times;[15] and the Chinookan-speaking Wasco and Wishram to the northwest in Oregon and Washington respectively.[16] East of the Wishram border (ca. 121°W), the north bank of the Columbia River was occupied in the main by the closely related Sahaptin-speaking Klickitat and probably also by a few Tenino.[17]

Local Groups

Aboriginally the Tenino were composed of four local groups or subtribes, each consisting typically of a pair of villages — one occupied in the winter months (November to March) and located at a protected interior site where water and wood for fuel were available, the other inhabited during the warmer months

---

Reprinted, by permission, from Murdock, G. P. 1980. The Tenino Indians. *Ethnology* 19:129-149.

and located at a site on the Columbia River or one of its tributaries where salmon fishing was especially productive. In several instances, however, a portion of a subtribe occupied a smaller secondary site during either the winter or the summer season. The four subgroups acknowledged their close interrelationship, and shifts in affiliation from one to another were not infrequent, whereas the bonds with other neighboring Sahaptin speakers, e.g., the Klickitat and Umatilla, were appreciably more tenuous. The four subtribes were the following:

Dalles Tenino. This group occupied two closely adjacent summer villages (#1 on the accompanying map) on the south bank of the Dalles of the Columbia and wintered on Eightmile Creek five miles to the south thereof. (It is important to distinguish the Dalles of the Columbia, also called Five Mile Rapids, from the modern town of The Dalles [Oregon], located several miles downstream to the west.) The name of the larger of the two summer settlements, _tinainu_, has come to apply to the tribe as a whole as well as to the Dalles subtribe.[18]

Tygh. This group had a summer village (#19) on the Deschutes River and its principal winter village (#14) on the site of modern Tygh Valley. Its territory had belonged originally to the Molala, who were expelled from it by the Dalles Tenino in a war estimated to have occurred shortly prior to 1830. It was occupied by the conquerors, but many of the latter continued to frequent the Dalles rather than the Deschutes River for the salmon season.

Wayam or _Deschutes_. This group had its summer village on the Columbia River at Celilo Falls (#2). Its winter village was located on the left bank of the Deschutes River (#3) just above its junction with the Columbia.

John Day. This group occupied the lower watershed of the John Day River with summer fishing villages (#7 and #8) on the south bank of the Columbia River and twin winter villages (#5 and #6) on either bank of the lower John Day River.

Warm Springs Reservation

In accordance with a treaty with the Indians of the region, dated June 25, 1855, the United States contracted to establish the Warm Springs Reservation. The bulk of the Tenino were removed thence in 1857, and the Wasco and kindred Chinookan peoples followed in 1858. Reservation records of 1858-59 report the presence of 850 Tenino on the reservation with about 60 Wayam and 100 John Day not yet established there, indicating a total population at that time of approximately 1,000 for the entire tribe. The neighboring Paiute, who were not settled on the reservation until a number of years later, were aggrieved because most of the land which it embraced had been traditionally theirs, and they retaliated by making periodic raids for horses and other booty against the Indians whom they considered intruders. The first Indian agent to be actually stationed on the reservation took charge on August 25, 1861. The first missionary, a United Presbyterian, arrived in 1892.

The data presented in this report derive almost exclusively from field work conducted by the writer among the reservation Tenino during periods of several weeks each in the summers of 1934 and 1935. His principal informants, with the dates of their births according to the records of the Warm Springs agency, were Mollie Mushingplaw (b. 1853), Annie Mary Quinn (b. 1850), Johnnie Quinn (b. 1835), Annie Scott (b. 1834), and Indian Spencer (b. 1837). Although all were born before the establishment of the reservation, three of them were young children at the time. Since data were sought primarily for the pre-reservation period, the author was fortunate in having two intelligent and observant individuals, who had been in their early twenties in 1857, available to check information received from the others, especially on the subjects of technology, subsistence economy, trade, social organization, and warfare. The data on religion were obtained mainly from Johnnie Quinn, the most prestigeful surviving shaman of the tribe, and thus probably pertain to a period several decades later than the rest.

Subsistence Economy

Prior to the reservation period the Tenino lived a semi-nomadic life, practicing no agriculture and possessing no domestic animals except dogs and at a later date a modest number of horses. They subsisted primarily by fishing but to an important extent also by hunting and gathering.[19] The men hunted and did most of the fishing. The women dried the meat, smoked the fish, and did most of the gathering, although the men helped in collecting acorns and pine nuts and to a lesser extent in picking berries.[20] The women conducted most of the trade with visitors from other tribes, the men confining themselves chiefly to the exchange of horses and an occasional distant trading expedition.

In their winter villages each family unit had two houses — an elliptical, semi-subterranean, earth-covered lodge used for sleeping and a rectangular frame dwelling with walls and a gable roof of tule mats used for cooking and daytime activities.[21] Winter pursuits included hunting and trapping, stream fishing, fuel gathering, and the manufacture of artifacts. In late March the Tenino dismantled their winter dwellings and removed to their summer villages. Here each family group erected a rectangular shed of poles and mats with a flat roof, of which half was used as living quarters and the other half for drying salmon.

In early April special parties were dispatched to gather roots and catch salmon for an important first-fruits ceremony.[22] Except for the John Day, who celebrated separately, the entire tribe assembled at a Dalles Tenino village. After this festival about half the families of a village departed for a series of expeditions toward the south; they lived for several days at a time in temporary camps of mat-covered tipis while the women gathered roots and the men hunted. The rest of the population remained in the summer village, catching and drying salmon. In July the entire population returned to the summer villages for another first-fruits ceremony, this one featuring berries and venison ritually obtained by a special party of six men and six women.

Following the summer festival the people again divided, part remaining in the villages to continue salmon fishing and to trade while the rest went to the Cascade Mountains to gather berries and nuts and to hunt. In September, at the conclusion of the berry season, hunting parties set out on long expeditions up the Deschutes and John Day rivers. The women smoked the meat obtained by the men and gathered late-ripening roots and berries. In October a special party collected tule reeds for mats. The drying sheds were now dismantled, and the people removed to their winter villages, reconditioning and occupying the dwellings there.

Trade

The region was one of the major foci for intertribal trade in aboriginal North America. An extensive network of trade relations, centering on the Tenino, Wasco, and Wishram villages on the Dalles of the Columbia, bound their inhabitants to the tribes inhabiting the Columbia River downstream to the coast and upstream to the edge of the Plains, as well as to the peoples in the heart of the Plateau to the north and those of southern Oregon and northeastern California to the South.[23] Parties of Tenino men occasionally undertook short trading expeditions in all directions, but in the main it was visitors from the surrounding tribes who brought their wares to the Dalles to exchange them for native products and imports from elsewhere.[24] The trading season reached its height in late summer when the salmon run began to slacken.

The visitors went from house to house, bartering with the local women. No form of true money was used, although strings of dentalium shells were widely accepted in exchange for other goods.

To this trade the Tenino contributed their own products — chiefly dried salmon, fish oil, and furs — and the goods they had obtained from other visitors. The principal imports were dentalia and other shells from the west; coiled baskets from the north; horses, buffalo hides, and parfleches from the east; and slaves, California baskets and beads, eagle feathers, and Pit River bows from the south. The Klamath, who mediated most of the commerce with the south, obtained dried salmon, dentalia, and horses in return for products brought from California. The Chinookan traders from the lower Columbia exchanged their shells for twined bags, bows, and skins. Trade from the north was mediated by the Wishram, who brought baskets and some horses in return for slaves, fish, and shells. Furs, hides, dentalia, bows, and dried fish were traded to the Umatilla for products obtained by the latter from tribes farther to the east.

A principal consequence of this extensive trade was widespread intertribal peace. Except for their war of conquest against the Molala[25] and one very minor skirmish with the Klamath, the Tenino have no memory of warfare with any of their neighbors save the Paiute, but conflict with this tribe, which significantly had little of value to trade, was endemic. On the whole, in contradiction to allegations by Teit, the Tenino in the pre-reservation period were expanding very gradually at the expense of the Paiute.

Villages, Camp Sites, and Trails

The accompanying map of Tenino territory, showing the location of their villages, major camping sites, and principal trails, is designed to clarify the annual round of economic activities. The map employs the following conventions: a heavy dashed line to indicate the crest of the Cascade Range; solid triangles for summer fishing villages; solid rectangles for winter villages and permanent settlements; open circles for overnight camp sites; and solid circles for sites occupied for somewhat longer periods for hunting, minor fishing, the gathering of roots, fruits, berries, etc. The seven principal trails in Tenino country are listed below by capital letters. The villages and major camping sites along each are indicated by numbers corresponding to those on the map.

A. An important trail along the south bank of the Columbia River, which ran from Wasco territory in the west to Umatilla country in the east and connected the principal settlements of the Dalles Tenino, Wayam, and John Day subtribes. Its continuation downstream led through Chinookan territory to the Pacific coast.

1. The paired summer villages of the Dalles Tenino. Here all the Tenino except the John Day subtribe foregathered annually for the spring and summer first-fruits festivals. From the principal village of the Wishram, on the opposite bank, connecting trails converged from the Salishan and Sahaptin tribes of central Washington.[26]

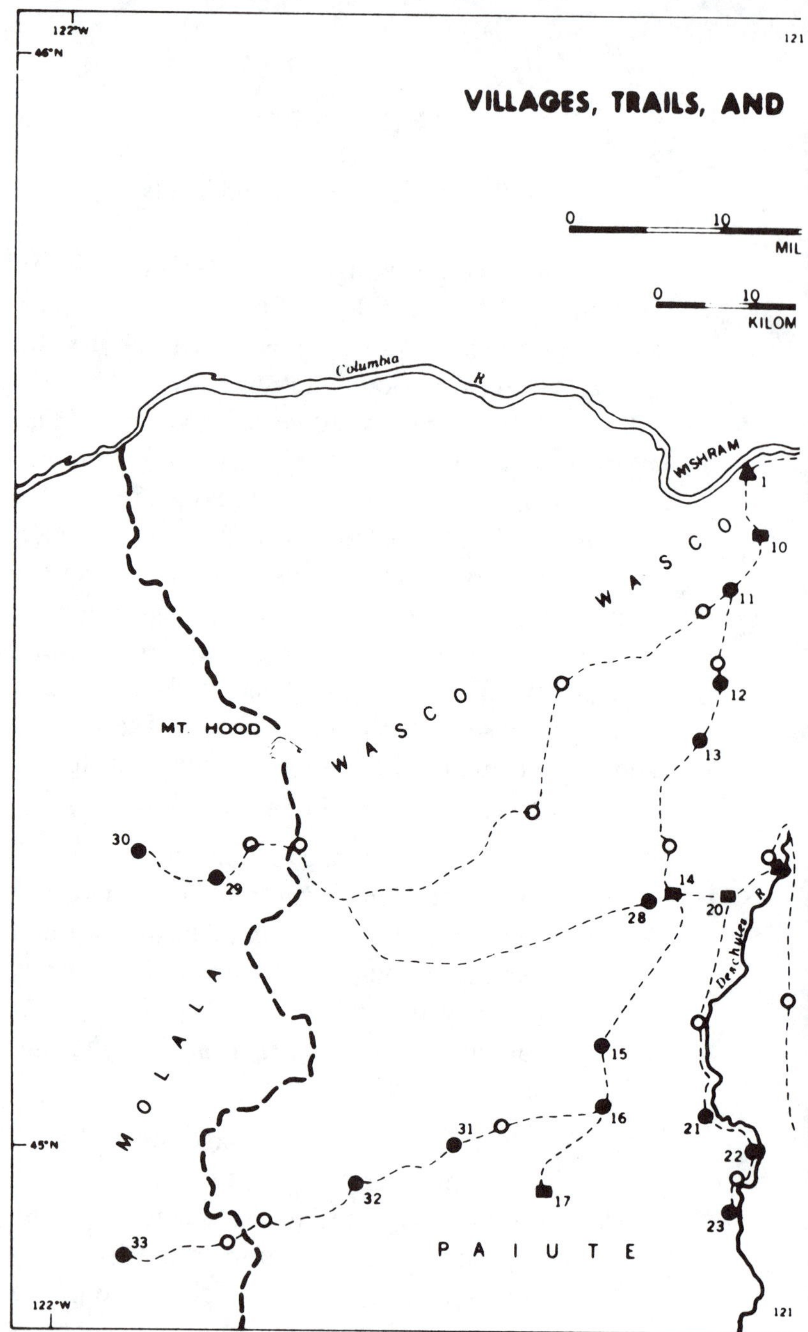

PLATE 6: Villages, Trails and Camp Sites of the Tenino. Interstate 84 runs along the Oregon shore of the Columbia River to Portland c. 100 miles distant.

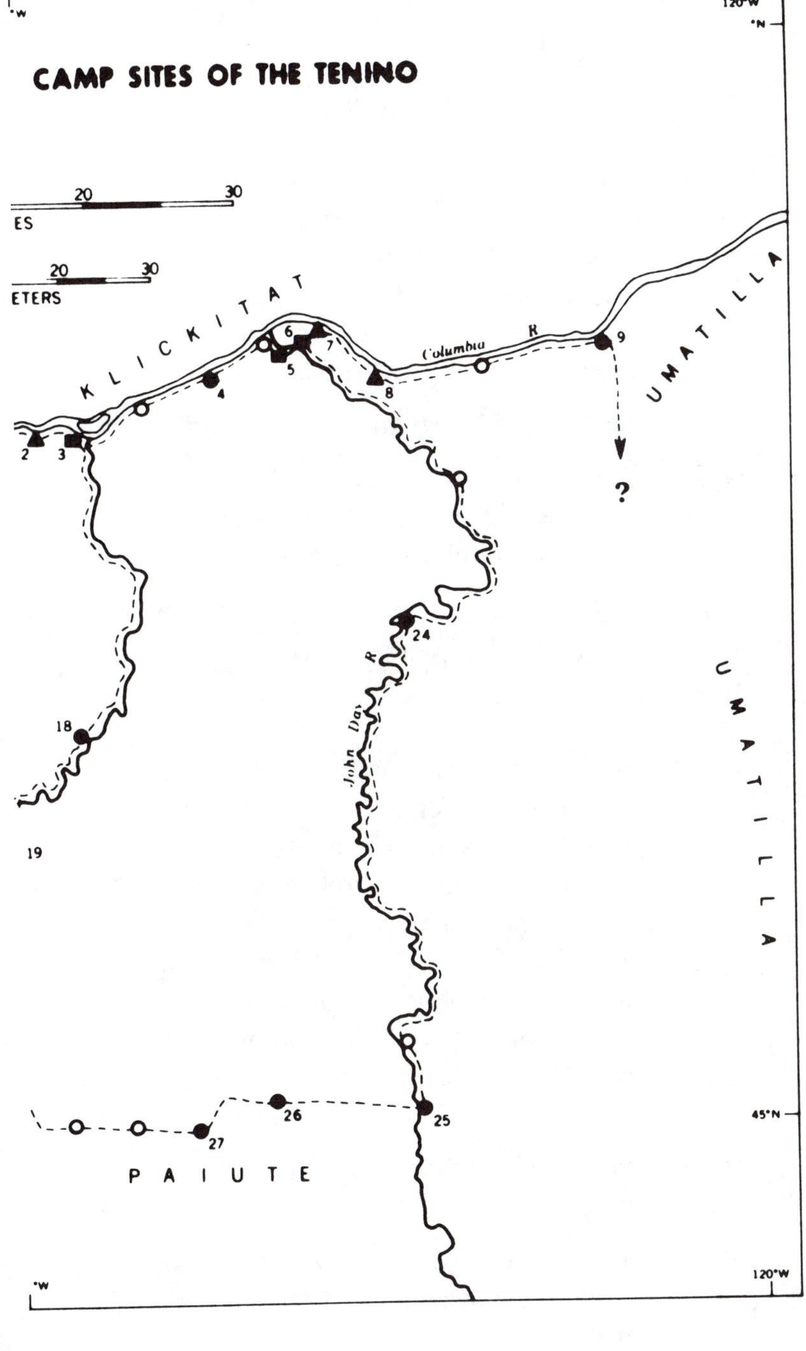

CAMP SITES OF THE TENINO
120°W
°W
°N
20
30
ES
20
30
ETERS
KLICKITAT
UMATILLA
Columbia R
John Day R
1
2
3
4
5
6
7
8
9
?
18
19
24
25
26
27
45°N
PAIUTE
UMATILLA

2. The summer village of the Wayam subtribe at Celilo Falls. Across the river a connecting trail led northwestward through Klickitat country to Mt. Adams, frequented for huckleberries in the late summer by the Wayam and John Day people.

3. The winter village of the Wayam subtribe.

4. Here, on the site of modern Rufus, travelers made brief stops to net salmon and gather roots or chokecherries in season.

5, 6. Winter villages of the John Day subtribe.

7, 8. Summer villages of the John Day subtribe.

9. A site, adjacent to Umatilla territory, frequented by the John Day people in the spring for roots and in the early fall for trade with the Umatilla. From here the trail continued eastward through alien territory to the edge of the Plains, and a connecting trail, branching off to the south but unfortunately not accurately located, was followed by John Day hunting parties in the late fall.

B. An important trail connecting the villages of the Dalles Tenino and Tygh subtribes.

10. The winter village of the Dalles Tenino, located five miles inland from their summer villages.

11. One of several sites in the vicinity visited briefly for chokecherries in season.

12. A site visited in early April to obtain hoops for dipnets preparatory to the fishing season, and again in July to gather hazelnuts.

13. An important site frequented by the Tygh and Dalles Tenino in the spring to gather roots and to hunt.

14. The principal winter village of the Tygh subtribe, located on the site of modern Tygh Valley, with a smaller satellite village a mile and a half to the southwest.

15, 16. Important centers for root gathering and incidental hunting in middle and late April.

17. The site of modern Simnasho, aboriginally a center for gathering roots and hawthorn berries but since 1857 the center of Tenino settlement on the Warm Springs Reservation. Immediately south lay Paiute country, traversed by a trail followed by Klamath trading parties on their way to the Dalles.

C. A trail following the course of the Deschutes River, connecting the territories of the Wayam and Tygh subtribes.

18. A temporary fishing village occupied by the Tygh people for several weeks in September.

19. The principal summer village of the Tygh subtribe. Its houses were located on either

side of the Deschutes River, which was crossed with the aid of a willow-bark rope stretched from bank to bank.

20. A small Tygh winter village.

21, 22. Hunting camps occupied for several days each in October.

23. The site of a hunting camp occupied for a week in the autumn to kill deer, antelope, and mountain sheep, which were driven into a blind V-shaped canyon, and to smoke the meat and prepare the hides. A special party of men returned in November to gather tule reeds, which were bundled into rafts and floated downstream to the villages on the Deschutes and Columbia rivers. The country south of this point was Paiute territory, but Tenino hunting parties sometimes visited it in force, even in pre-reservation days.

D. A trail leading upstream from the John Day villages along the east bank of the John Day River.

24. A site visited by the John Day people in the spring for roots and in the autumn for hunting and the gathering of chokecherries and late-ripening roots.

25. An important site regularly visited by the John Day people in both spring and late summer, even during periods of hostilities with the Paiute, who disputed its possession and controlled the country farther south.

E. An east-west trail skirting the southern edge of Tenino territory and connecting the upper John Day country with that of the Tygh subtribe.

26. An important site visited by the John Day people in May to tap the abundant root resources of the region.

27. The most important of a number of sites in the Shaniko region visited by the Tygh, Wayam, and Dalles Tenino in May and June to gather roots and hunt antelope and mule deer. This was a festive season when camp life was punctuated by gambling and religious ceremonies.

F. Connecting trails from the Dalles Tenino and Tygh villages to the berrying grounds southwest of Mt. Hood.

28. A salt lick kept under regular surveillance by the Tygh people and visited by a party of hunters whenever elk were spotted there.

29. The first of a series of berrying grounds on the slopes of Mt. Hood. Parties left the villages after the berry festival in late July to gather huckleberries and pine nuts, hunt deer and elk, and lay in a supply of dried berries and smoked meat for the winter.

30. The largest of the berrying grounds of the region. Parties remained for several weeks, returning to the villages in October.

G. A trail from the Tygh country to the huckleberry grounds around Olallie Butte, utilized by the Tygh people after their displacement of the Molala.

31, 32. Sites visited just before the berry festival for camas roots, which were abundant in the vicinity, and after the ceremony by parties on their way to the berrying grounds.

33. A prolonged stay was made here in middle and late summer to gather huckleberries and to hunt and lay in a supply of meat.

Technology

Since Ray (1942) has published an inventory of Tenino artifacts, the material culture will be treated here from the point of its utilization of the materials provided by the environment. Noteworthy is the extremely limited use made of mineral products. Metal-working and the ceramic arts, for example, were unknown, as were both the grinding and chipping of stone. A seeming exception was the use of obsidian flakes as knives and projectile points, but informants insisted that these were obtained from the habitation sites of an earlier population along the Columbia, where they were allegedly deposited by Raven, and were never manufactured by the Tenino themselves. The Tenino put unworked stones to such minor uses as damming small streams for fish and as sinkers for fishing lines and nets, but they never employed stone in dwelling construction. The sole shaping technique was "pecking," used mainly in fashioning pestles for grinding food,[27] mauls for splitting firewood, and hammers for excavating dugout canoes.

Animal products were much more widely used in the manufacture of artifacts. The horns of deer, elk, and mountain sheep and goats supplied the materials for wedges, picks, chisels, net gauges, gambling dice, and projectile points.[28] The long bones of deer were made into large fishing gorges, the points and barbs for fish spears, and awls and needles to sew mats and buckskin clothing. Small gorges were fashioned from rabbit bones, fishhooks from the nasal bones of deer, and skin scrapers from elk ribs. Deer sinews were made into sewing thread and bowstrings and were used as a reinforcement for bows. Eagle plumes served as feathers for arrows[29] and as decorations for ceremonial costumes, and brooms or brushes were fashioned from pelican feathers. Cordage and rope made from horsehair were employed as fishing lines and as hobbles, halters, tethers, and hitching lines for horses.

Animal skins constituted a major technological resource. The untanned hides of deer and elk provided tumplines or pack straps, thongs for stitching clothing and bedding, the mesh for snowshoes, nooses to trap beaver, ropes to lasso horses, drumheads, bags for collecting roots and for storing clothing, water, and deer tallow, and the shields and cuirasses worn by leading warriors. The dried skins of black and grizzly bears were used as floor rugs and sleeping mattresses, and the tanned pelts of the wolf, coyote, cougar, lynx, otter, beaver, and raccoon were employed as bedding. A buckskin bag stuffed with hair or feathers served as a pillow. All clothing except the basketry caps worn by women was made of skins — the tanned hides of deer, mountain sheep, antelope, and cow elk with the hair removed for men's shirts, women's dresses, and the belts of both sexes; tanned deerskin with the hair on for men's breechclouts and caps and for the leggings and winter robes of both sexes; tanned and smoked buckskin for men's and women's moccasins;[30] and tanned furs of coyotes and rabbits for winter socks, mittens, and mufflers. In addition, blankets sewn from strips of rabbit skin served both as bedding and as robes in exceptionally cold weather.[31]

Wood was used for a wide variety of artifacts, of which only representative examples can be cited. Cedar was employed for dugout canoes and paddles; cottonwood for house timbers and fishing scaffolds; oak or comparable hard woods for bow staves, digging sticks, excavating shovels, and war clubs;[32] fir for dip-net handles, fish-spear shafts, fire drills, and war spears; maple for the foreshafts of fish spears; hazel for dip-net hoops and snowshoes frames; serviceberry wood for arrow shafts; pine for netting needles; wild rose stems for needles to sew mats and for cradle hoops; juniper for the hoops of drums; willow for fishing rods and for lashing timbers in various structures; elder stalks for whistles to call deer; and the light stems of an unidentified shrub with a pithy core for needles, the slabs of slat armor, and an implement for dredging clams. Utensils of wood, such as dishes, spoons, and mortars, came into use only after European contact.

A number of vegetal fibers and strands supplemented horsehair, deer sinews, rawhide thongs, and strips of rabbit skins as materials for the textile arts — for thread, cordage, mats, nets, baskets, and bags. The most important were the fibers of the inner bark of the willow, the dried stems of a jointed swamp grass, and strips of the outer bark of manzanita. Simple plaited mats were used for the construction of fish weirs, but all other mats were either sewn or twined. Various types of sewn mats of tule or cattail rushes were used for the roofs, walls, and doors of dwellings, for floor coverings, and for spreading roots and berries to dry. Twined mats were made for a number of specialized purposes — of willow-bark fibers for mattresses, of manzanita bark for roofing, and of swamp grass for drying salmon and as doors for pit dwellings. Mats were tied together and lashed to house timbers with cord of braided manzanita bark. Nets of all kinds, including fishing seines and nets to catch rabbits, were made of willow-bark cord by means of a netting needle and a net gauge.[33]

Of all the artifacts of a Tenino household, items of basketry were the most numerous. With the exception of simple carrying baskets sewn from cedar bark or made by doubling a cattail mat and sewing the edges, all baskets were the product of two techniques of manufacture — coiling and twining. Coiled baskets were used for picking, carrying, and storing berries, and a watertight variety served as containers for liquids and for boiling with the aid of hot stones. Though numerous, they were not manufactured by the Tenino themselves but were obtained exclusively by trade with the tribes north of the Columbia River.[34] Artifacts of twined basketry fell into three principal categories: (a) rigid baskets, including fish traps, cradles, sieves, and trays for scraping the skins from roots; (b) semi-flexible baskets, including carrying and storage baskets, women's hats, and basketry mortars; and (c) flexible baskets or bags of two-ply twining, usually with a buckskin drawstring around the rim, used principally for carrying and storing. Specialized baskets, e.g., a type used in the stick game, were obtained in trade with the south. Despite their expertise in basketry, neither the Tenino nor their neighbors were familiar with either the loom weaving or finger weaving of cloth in any form.

Division of Labor

Specialization was primarily by sex, with a distribution of tasks that appears entirely equitable. The men, in addition to hunting, trapping, fishing, and waging war, manufactured practically all the artifacts employed in these activities. They did all work in stone, bone, and horn. They felled trees, cut and split wood, brought in timber and firewood, and manufactured all wooden implements, including those used by women. They made and paddled the dugout canoes, wove nets, and manufactured all musical implements. They also did most of the work of house construction, including the excavation of pit dwellings, the raising of house timbers, and the attachment of mats for all structures except the tipi. Women, however, dug the post holes. There was a definite tendency to reserve the more difficult crafts to men who were too old to hunt.

The women did most of the gathering, although men collected tule reeds and nuts.[35] The women also smoked meat, dried fish and berries, and prepared and cooked the food. They tanned and prepared all skins except elk hides, and made, repaired, and laundered all clothing and bedding. They manufactured thread, cordage, mats, baskets, and bags, monopolizing the textile arts except for the preparation of rope, nets, and fish traps. In addition, they did the housework — cleaning the dwellings, sweeping the mats, and airing the bedding — and assumed primary care of the younger children. Both sexes carried burdens. Men brought in game, timber, and firewood with the aid of a packstrap across the chest. Women fetched roots, berries, and fish in pack baskets supported by a tumpline on the forehead.

There were no full-time specialized occupations. The division of labor by sex was matter-of-fact and by no means rigid. The men had no objection to cooking for themselves on hunting or military expeditions and readily helped the women in certain of their tasks, especially in berry picking. Nor did the women resent fetching firewood when a man was not available. One female informant was even admired, as a young woman, for her expertise in catching beavers by diving into their lodges — a task ordinarily associated with the male sex. Another woman gained fame when, waylaid by a Paiute warrior, she stout-heartedly defended herself with her digging stick, slew him, and proudly returned to camp with his scalp as a trophy.

Household Organization

Economic factors found a clear reflection in the composition of the Tenino household, which, with occasional exceptions, included the families of two adult married men.[36] The two families slept on opposite sides of the semi-subterranean winter dwelling and shared the adjacent frame living house, where they maintained a single common hearth and cooked and ate together. The same joint family also maintained a shed dwelling in the summer village, although ordinarily only one of the component families was resident there throughout the season. The other was absent from the village most of the time on spring root-gathering trips, summer berry-picking excursions, and the autumn hunt, but it shared the shed residence during the two annual first-fruits festivals and on the brief intervals between trips. Oftentimes the two families would alternate on expeditions away from home, but sometimes, especially when one man was much older or less active than the other, his family would remain at the fishing village throughout the summer season. Occasionally the families would divide equally the salmon, game, roots, and berries which either had obtained, but more commonly the sharing was achieved indirectly through the common table at which both, during the winter months, consumed the products which both had accumulated during the preceding summer season.[37]

The owner of the dwelling, usually but not always the eldest male occupant, was the head of the household. The other adult male was usually his married son or younger brother but was occasionally a sister's or daughter's husband or even a remote relative or an unrelated friend. A son, when he married, usually continued to reside with his father, at least for a time, but if the house became overcrowded he joined a brother or other relative to build a new dwelling and establish an independent joint household. Alternatively, if there was room in the house of his wife's father or brother, particularly if the latter was wealthy and personally congenial, he might reside matrilocally with him, but this solution seems to have been somewhat exceptional. On the death of the owner, the dwelling was inherited by his household partner if a near relative, otherwise by his eldest child or next young sibling resident in the community.

Marriage

Marriages were usually arranged at the instance of the young man but occasionally of his parents, whose permission was always required. In either case, his father selected an old man to act as go-between and to visit the bride's parents to secure their consent to the union.[38] Boys typically married at about twenty years of age, girls at between fifteen and eighteen. Local exogamy was preferred and usual, but marriages within the village were not prohibited.[39] Unions even occurred fairly frequently with members of neighboring tribes with whom the Tenino maintained friendly trade relations. Incest taboos, governing sex as well as marriage, extended bilaterally to all close consanguineal kinsmen.

Weddings ranked with the two annual first-fruits festivals as major ceremonial occasions in Tenino life. They involved an elaborate exchange of presents between the close relatives of the bride and the groom. The festivities were held shortly after betrothal at the bride's village, outside of which the groom's party set up a tipi camp.[40] The parties were headed respectively by the groom's father and the bride's mother.[41] If either were dead, his place was taken by the other parent or by some other senior relative of either sex. Each was represented by a spokesman, an old man who was not a close relative.

The ceremony began with a visit by the spokesman for the groom's father to the village of the bride. He carried a bundle of sticks, each representing a horse offered as a gift by a man or woman of his party.[42] These he presented to the bride's mother, describing each horse in detail. After choosing one for herself, she called upon the members of her party individually, in order of their nearness of kinship to the bride, to select an animal and thereby assume the obligation to engage in a series of reciprocal prestations with its donor. In this manner the participants on both sides became divided into pairs of trading partners. Informants insisted that such pairs were not necessarily of the same sex.

There ensued a series of visits alternately to the bride's relatives at her village and to the groom's relatives at his camp. On each of these the members of the visiting party brought gifts for their trading partners and were entertained at a feast. The presentations made by the groom's relatives and the food served at the feasts given by them consisted of items produced by or associated with the male role in the division of labor by sex, particularly — in addition to horses — animal skins and furs, venison, and salmon. Conversely the bride's kinsmen, regardless of sex, contributed products of feminine industry — buckskin clothing, ornaments, mats, twined bags, roots, and berries. (For details, see Murdock 1958:304-306). The bride and groom themselves were merely onlookers at the feasts and prestations, receiving only speeches of good advice. The goods presented to the bride's relatives were admittedly of somewhat greater value because of the inclusion of horses, but informants insisted that the transaction was a genuine exchange with no overtones of a brideprice.[43]

The Tenino practiced polygyny. It occurred with moderate frequency and was by no means confined to men of wealth and high status.[44] Five wives was the maximum number in any instance remembered by informants. A man might take his wife's younger sister as a secondary spouse, but this was neither preferential nor particularly common.[45] Co-wives lived in the same dwelling and shared household tasks, but the first wife enjoyed a somewhat higher status. The husband slept with each in rotation. A widow was expected to marry one of the brothers of her deceased husband, and was permitted to choose among them, but she might marry another man if she chose.[46] The sororate was more strongly preferential, and indeed almost obligatory, for the unmarried sister of a deceased wife. The elaborate property exchanges were customary only for a first marriage; subsequent unions involved merely a few gifts.

Marriages were relatively stable, and divorce was rare. Either spouse, however, could terminate a union on grounds of adultery, childlessness, or incompatibility. Young children went with their mother unless she had deserted her husband, in which case they were cared for by their father's mother. Boys over ten years of age, and sometimes older girls as well, remained with or returned to their father.

Kinship

Kinship was reckoned bilaterally. The Tenino lacked clans, moieties, and any other type of unilinear kin group. The only corporate groups were the nuclear and polygynous family, the joint household, and the local community. Definite recognition, however, was accorded to one non-corporate grouping of kinsmen — the bilateral kindred — which varied in composition from individual to individual and included, for any particular person, all those to whom he could trace a specific consanguineal connection in any line. It excluded affinal relatives but regularly embraced second cousins and often third cousins as well. It functioned particularly in life-crisis ceremonies, notably the property exchanges at weddings described above.

The Tenino system of kinship nomenclature included 40 distinct terms. Since these have been listed and defined by Murdock (1958:308-310), and an almost identical system has been reported by Jacobs (1932) for the closely related Upper Cowlitz and Klickitat tribes in Washington, it will suffice here to present merely a succinct classificatory analysis. There were (1) six terms for siblings, extending to both cross and parallel cousins throughout the kindred, distinguishing those older than the speaker by sex only and those younger by both sex and the sex of the speaker; (2) four grandparental terms, distinguishing the father's from the mother's parents of each sex and used self-reciprocally for grandchildren as well; (3) four terms for parents' siblings, distinguishing those of either parent both from the parent and from each other as well as by sex; (4) six terms for nephews and nieces, distinguished by the sex of the speaker and the sex of the connecting relative in all cases and also by the sex of the relative in the case of a male but not a female speaker; (5) three terms for parents-in-law, also used self-reciprocally for children-in-law, the wife's parents being distinguished from the husband's and also, unlike the latter, by sex; (6) four terms for siblings-in-law, those of opposite sex being differentiated according to whether the connecting relative was alive or dead and those of the same sex by the sex of both speaker and relative; and (7) two special terms for father's sister's husband — remarkable as the only exceptions to strict bilateral symmetry — differing according to the sex of the speaker and also applied self-reciprocally to the wife's brothers' children. A final characteristic was an extensive differentiation of vocative from referential forms, the former reflecting different roots in about half of all cases.

An unexpected product of the field work was the discovery of a series of explicit patterns of behavior prevailing between kinsmen of particular categories. One such special relationship was that between a paternal grandfather and his son's son. The former was responsible for instilling physical hardihood and military virtues in his grandson. It was customary for him, during the boyhood of the latter, to undress and whip him, to roll him naked in the snow, to make him lie in the bed of an icy stream, and to subject him to comparable hardening ordeals. The motivation was purely educational. No notion of joking or horseplay was involved, and the boy made no effort to retaliate, either at the time or in later life.[47]

No comparable behavior patterns were discoverable between paternal or maternal uncles or aunts and their nephews or nieces. Attitudes and conduct toward parents-in-law and children-in-law were modeled on those between parents and children, and showed no evidence of avoidance or special reserve. The relationship between brothers was affectionate and co-operative and was particularly close if they maintained a common household. Between brother and sister, however, there prevailed a measure of restraint and avoidance. They could not sleep in a house alone, nor walk, ride, or sit together unless someone else was present.

Brothers-in-law maintained a friendly and co-operative relationship resembling that between brothers. When a man built a house, for example, he expected his brothers-in-law to lend assistance without anticipation of payment. A special privilege enjoyed by a sibling-in-law of either sex was that of claiming a valuable possession belonging to any person thus related to him. The claimant was obligated only to return a similar object of lesser value. Between siblings-in-law of opposite sex there prevailed a relationship of considerable intimacy, though not of permitted joking.

Even sexual intercourse between them was common, and seems to have been taken almost for granted. During one interview, for example, both the informant and the interpreter readily confessed to having had sex relations with the sisters of their wives.

Perhaps the most striking example of pattern kinship behavior was that prevailing between a father's sister's husband and his wife's brother's children. These relatives, as noted above, called each other by special self-reciprocal kinship terms, which were not balanced by corresponding special terminology for and by the spouses of other siblings of the parents. The associated behavior was equally distinctive. A boy or young man fetched firewood and did other chores for the husband of his paternal aunt but recognized no similar obligation toward the spouses of his other parents' siblings. A girl or woman likewise regarded the tie with her father's sister's husband as especially close. The most characteristic feature of the relationship, however, was the licensed joking which it entailed. A person poked fun and cracked jokes freely at the expense of a father's sister's husband or wife's brother's child, and such a relative submitted with good nature and retaliated in kind, knowing that no offense was intended. Rough practical jokes were permitted and expected when both relatives were males, whereas between opposite sexes the joking was largely verbal in character.

Social Stratification

The Tenino not only engaged in the slave trade but practiced slavery themselves to a limited extent. Informants estimated the number of slaves kept by the tribe in the immediate pre-contact period at about 25, with three being the largest number held by a single owner.[48] The Tenino captured some slaves in their endemic warfare with the Paiute—exclusively women and children since male captives were invariably slain. A larger number, however, were obtained by purchase from the Klamath; these were partly of Modoc but mainly of Achomawi-Atsugewi origin. Whatever their provenience, most slaves were passed on in trade to the north. Those who were retained lived in the houses of their masters and participated in ordinary household activities. Slave status was not hereditary, and captive children when they grew up ordinarily married Tenino and acquired their freedom, though they never fully lost the stigma of their slave origin.

Wealth distinctions were recognized, but they had not become crystallized into formal social classes as among the neighboring tribes of the Northwest Coast.[49] Most marriages, to be sure, occurred between families of comparable means, but unions between rich and poor were neither particularly frowned upon nor uncommon.

Chiefship

The Tenino lacked any form of political organization which transcended the limits of the local community. Each village had a recognized headman, who tended to be succeeded by his eldest son.[50] He was always a wealthy man and usually had several wives. His dwelling in the winter village was larger than that of other men, and he was expected to be generous in giving feasts. He was assisted by subchiefs, usually two in number, who acted as his councillors, messengers, and spokesmen. He advised in the planning of a military expedition but rarely led or even accompanied a war party. He presided at popular assemblies called to discuss judicial cases, issues of war and peace, and other matters of general concern, but he exercised only negligible decision-making power. His most conspicuous function was that of haranguing his people every morning, noon, and evening on matters of conduct and morals. In general, social control was effected far more by informal mechanisms, such as the avoidance of public disapproval and the fear of retaliatory sorcery, than by means which might be considered more strictly legal or political.[51]

The Supernatural Environment

To the Tenino, the environment included a great deal that did not meet the eye. In addition to its physical aspects, it was populated by supernatural entities of various kinds—mysterious, often powerful or dangerous, and usually invisible except on occasion by shamans. Among these were the personal souls which animated the bodies of living men and women and were capable of absenting themselves for brief periods. After death, these souls departed permanently and normally went to a spirit world in the west, where they continued to live a life much like that on earth. Under certain circumstances, however, the disembodied souls of the dead lingered on near their graves or former haunts in the form of ghosts, which were capable of frightening and sometimes injuring the living.[52]

Other spiritual beings included mythical dwarfs and monsters, a Cannibal Woman who was invoked to frighten naughty children, and a trickster, Coyote, who was the subject of innumerable droll folk tales. There were also a variety of nature spirits who were identified with inanimate objects and such natural phenomena as winds, clouds, thunder, and fire. Much the most important of these were animal spirits. There were generic spirits for practically every species of wild animal. Each had specific characteristics generalized from those ascribed to the animal itself, and each controlled some particular type or types of superhuman power and was capable of conveying it to human beings. These powers included invulnerability to injuries in war, control over the weather, the ability to cure illness, skill in hunting and fishing, luck in gambling, and many others which the unaided human being lacked but earnestly coveted. The cultural means by which mankind gained access to these powers was, as in many other aboriginal North American societies, the spirit quest.[53]

Spirit Quest

At the age of six or a little older, every child, male or female, was sent out at night into the wilderness in search of a guardian spirit, and this procedure was repeated from time to time until the child had accumulated five such spirits as lifelong helpers.[54] He did not venture out unprepared but was instructed by an experienced old man or woman where to go, what to expect, and how to behave, i.e., to construct piles of rocks and keep alert. Moreover, he was already familiar with the distinctive actions and songs of most of the spirits he was likely to encounter from observation of the spirit dances held annually in a special dance house in the winter village. At these dances, which lasted five days, all adults danced in imitation of the behavior of their guardian spirits and sang the songs appropriate to each, and novices were initiated under the tutelage of an experienced shaman.

With his anxieties and sensory perceptions heightened by the darkness and the very real dangers of his situation, the child was prepared to magnify the dim shadows and rustlings in the bush and to construe them in terms of his expectations. They would gradually crystallize into a vision of a human figure speaking the Tenino language — for it was always thus that a spirit addressed a seeker. In revealing itself to the child, the spirit would utter its characteristic animal cry, sing its special spirit song, explain the specific power it was conferring and how to evoke and employ it, and finally resume its animal form and disappear.[55] The power offered could not be rejected or revealed to others, on penalty of punishment or its loss, but the successful seeker was expected to sing his spirit song and dance his spirit dance at the next winter ceremony. In this manner people became aware of the spirit helpers of their neighbors, but only in a general way of the powers they controlled.

Shamans

Every adult Tenino made use of the limited number of supernatural powers received from his guardian spirits to advance his own personal interests. Certain individuals, however, controlled an exceptionally wide range of such powers, became specialists in the magical arts, and were charged with the responsibility of employing them for socially approved goals. These were the shamans. Women as well as men could become shamans, and they were not considered inferior in power though they were appreciably fewer in number.

A person became a shaman if, after puberty and the conclusion of his spirit quests, he discovered that other spirits were attracted to him.[56] These were the former guardians of deceased people, especially of dead shamans, who were conceived as "hungry" and eager to attach themselves to a new master who would "feed" them. Unlike ordinary people, who were limited to five supernatural helpers, shamans accumulated a wider variety and much larger number of such. Moreover, a prospective shaman had to pass the equivalent of a state medical board examination conducted by the shamans who had already been admitted to practice. They carefully reviewed his credentials, especially his reputation for personal integrity, and required him to demonstrate his control over his spirits. Since only shamans, it was believed, could see and hear the guardian spirits of other people, they alone were qualified to test the neophyte's professional competence and to reject possibly fraudulent claims.[57]

Once he was accepted by his senior colleagues, the young shaman could begin to practice. For his first five cases, however, he could accept no fees. Thereafter he was generously rewarded with gifts, which, however, he received only if, and after, his ministrations proved successful. Shamans sometimes assisted one another, but they exhibited no formal organization except in the examination of neophytes.

The principal social function of the shaman was the cure of illness by magical means. The Tenino ascribed most disease to spirit possession — to the invasion of the patient's body by an animal or other spirit projected thence by real or imagined sorcery.[58] Shamans alone had the power, with the aid of their spirit helpers, to exorcise such intrusive spirits and thereby restore the patient to health. Hence, when a person fell ill and did not respond to lay treatment, his family summoned a shaman to his bedside and assembled his kinsmen and friends, who provided an accompaniment for the ensuing seance by singing and beating time with sticks on a dry log.

To effect a cure, it was first necessary for the shaman to identify the specific supernatural agent responsible for the ailment. This he accomplished with the aid of a special diagnostic spirit, of which every shaman controlled at least one — that of some naturally curious animal such as a magpie. After preliminaries such as washing his hands, blowing on a coiled basket of water, and sprinkling the patient, he summoned the spirit by singing its special song and projecting it into the patient's body through a tube. After a brief period, during which the diagnostic spirit supposedly explored the interior of the body, it returned to the mouth of the shaman and informed him of the identity of the intrusive spirit. Occasionally a diagnostic spirit would report, not the presence of an intrusive spirit, but the absence of the patient's own soul. To cope with such exceptional cases of soul loss, a shaman's retinue of spirit helpers included, in addition to animal spirits, at least one human ghost, who could be dispatched to the spirit world to fetch back the wandering soul.[59]

In the usual case, however, the diagnostic spirit indicated than an alien animal spirit was in possession of the patient's body. The shaman then summoned one of his spirit helpers with a power considered greater than that of the invading spirit. The powers of the various animal spirits were graded and scaled with reference to one another in terms of projections from the innate or traditional characteristics of the natural animals themselves. Thus, the grizzly spirit, one of the strongest of all, enjoyed ascendancy over most other animal spirits but not over that of the rattlesnake, which, in turn yielded ascendancy to certain bird spirits, including the eagle. A shaman could hope to exorcise a spirit possessing a patient only with the aid of a spirit helper with superior power. If he did not control such a spirit, he withdrew from the case, for otherwise he would have lost the ensuing contest and with it his life.

Having summoned an appropriate spirit helper, the shaman blew it into the patient's body, precipitating a spectacular struggle with the invading spirit in which the shaman and the patient were violently tossed about. When the possessing spirit began to weaken, the shaman sucked it into his mouth, spat it into his cupped hands, and, after renewed convulsions, plunged it into his basket of water to give it its final quietus. Then, with a puff of breath, he sent both the victor and the loser back to their proper places in nature (for further details, see Murdock 1965).[60]

Implicit in the shaman's power to cure by magical means was his power to kill through sorcery. He could dispatch a spirit helper to take possession of another person's body and thereby cause him to fall ill and, unless saved by the timely intervention of another shaman, to die. While suspicion of sorcery was certainly far more common than its actual practice, this unquestionably did occur. It was considered entirely legitimate in warfare, and it seems to have been employed against in-group members in extremities when other means of social control or punishment had failed. It was presumably this possibility which accounted for the unusual precautions taken by the Tenino to admit to shamanistic practice only persons of upright character and sound judgment, who could be trusted to use the powers entrusted to them in a thoroughly responsible manner.[61]

The Prophet Dance

The Tenino have long been involved in the Plateau millenarian movement known as the Prophet Dance and, since at least the early reservation period, in its distinctive Sahaptin derivative, the Smohalla cult. The history and characteristics of this movement have been reviewed by Spier (1935). In 1934 the Smohalla cult was still the prevailing religion of the Tenino; only an insignificant handful of families had accepted either Christianity or the nativistic Shaker or Feather cults. Unfortunately, however, informants were extremely reluctant to discuss either the theology or the forms of worship of the cult, presumably because of its anti-White orientation, and hence little can be added to the information supplied to and published by Spier (1935).

Basically the cult was based on an old, and presumably in part aboriginal belief in the imminent destruction of the world and its renewal through the return of the dead to a happier life on earth. This day could be hastened by the observance of strict moral precepts and by fervent dancing of what purported to be the dances of the dead. From time to time a series of prophets of various tribes allegedly died and returned to the land of the living bringing testimony to the truth of the doctrine and conveying supplementary revelations. The principal late prophet was Smohalla, a Sahaptin from Priest Rapids in Central Washington, who traveled widely through the Plateau bearing the old message foretelling the resurrection of the dead with the added prediction of the disappearance of the Whites and the restoration to the Indians of their former lands.

Among the Tenino this cult absorbed and partially transformed the aboriginal eschatology and funeral ceremonial and altered the form and rationale of the spring and summer first-fruits rituals. When witnessed in 1934, for example, the traditional summer berry festival was held in a special elongated wooden dance shed and consisted primarily of a stereotyped dance of typical Prophet Dance style in which the participants danced counterclockwise around the shed with hopping steps to the right and with right arms flexed in front, pausing but hopping in place after each circumference to encourage sinners to confess their sins.[62]

Associated with this form of the Prophet Dance, in addition to various features of myth and ritual of unmistakably aboriginal origin, were others clearly derived from Christianity, such as grace before meals, the observance of Sunday, belief in a High God referred to by an expression translatable as "Our Heavenly Father," and a conception of a last judgment and the physical resurrection of the dead.[63] Notable for their absence, however, were any traces of a divine Savior, of any conception of the Trinity, or of any ritual resembling the Mass — the very features most likely to have been inculcated in any direct contact with either Catholic or Protestant missionaries. Their borrowing must therefore have been indirect, and Spier (1935) makes a plausible case for their derivation at third or fourth hand from a group of Iroquois Indians of the Handsome Lake persuasion who migrated west and settled among the Flathead tribe of Western Montana around 1820.

PLATE 7: Umatilla River mouth, looking northward toward the Columbia River and hills on the Washington side. The modern town of Umatilla, Oregon, sprawls on both banks of the river. Photo by author.

PLATE 8: Two Umatilla infants in cradleboards. Maj. Lee Moorehouse photo, c. 1898.

PLATE 9: Umatilla child. Edw. S. Curtis photo, c. 1910.

PLATE 10: A Umatilla maid. Edw. S. Curtis photo, c. 1910.

PLATE 11: Umatilla women smoketanning buckskin.
Maj. Lee Moorehouse photo, c. 1898-1903.

PART THREE

THE UMATILLA INDIANS

I. INTRODUCTORY NOTES

The Umatilla Indians belonged to the Shahaptian division of the Shapwailautan linguistic stock. They lived on or about the mouth of the Umatilla River where it joins the Columbia River. The Indians' tribal name occurs over the region: the Umatilla River, Umatilla County, the city of Umatilla, also the Umatilla Indian Reservation. No large tribe, in 1910 according to the census they numbered 272; the U.S. Indian Office Report for 1923 counted 145; and the Indian Office Report for 1937 counted 124. As a result of the treaties of 1855 between Isaac Stevens and the region's Indian nations, the Umatillas were placed on a separate reservation near present-day Pendleton, Oregon.

The Umatilla's tribal location lies ca. 80 miles east of the Deschutes River mouth and the site of the Tenino Indians' villages. Like that country the land of the Umatillas is essentially flat, but sere and treeless. The climate includes hot, dry summers, and cold winters with some snow. And the river area probably contributed strong winds to their area. Thus, the Umatillas clustered about the sheltering dish or basin about the Umatilla River's mouth. There, especially at the wide and shallow mouth of the Umatilla River, migrating and spawning salmon might be easily caught, to feed and to sustain village life.

Unlike the Klickitats or the Wishrams who lived across the rapids-choked Columbia River and were thus naturally protected, the Umatillas were vulnerable to the warlike, maurauding Bannocks and Paiutes. We know little of Umatilla social and material culture. We assume that they must have lived lives subject to the same influences as their neighbors, the Teninos. And their lifestyles were, thus, probably similar to that of the Teninos, or even the Wascos, the Wishrams.

The tales included hereafter comprise an exciting, an important find. If brief, this sampling of Umatilla oral traditional literature was collected far enough back in time to be highly authentic. The literature allows a look, however brief, into the mental life of the tribe. We have scant hope that hitherto unpublished documents on tribal life from about the turn of the century might yet be discovered.

PLATE 12: Cayuse mother and child. Edw. S. Curtis photo, c. 1910.

PLATE 13: Cayuse woman. Edw. S. Curtis photo, c. 1910.

PLATE 14: Cayuse type. Edw. S. Curtis photo, c. 1910.

PLATE 15: A Cayuse girl with her proudly decked horse. Edw. S. Curtis photo, c. 1910.

PLATE 16: A Cayuse warrior. Edw. S. Curtis photo, c. 1910.

II. TALES OF THE UMATILLA INDIANS

4A. TESTING THE GREAT *TAH* POWER OF THE WARRIOR[64]

It was around Walla Walla, or in the Umatilla country,[65] that a warrior lived in an earlier day when the *Tah* was more powerful than now. He had a great powerful *Tah* and often went to the buffalo country alone, went among all the tribes wherever they were living. He said, "Indian war is a custom. I will go steal something to bring home. I shall become a chief sometime."

This was about all that he did, going on the warpath. He left his wife at home as he went to the forest to the enemy camp. He had many close escapes. He took horses, buffalo robes, dried meat and brought all to his home. He would bring horses of different colors, giving all of them to his friends and relations. Then he would go again. He grew wiser about how to find and bring away the best horses of the enemy tribes. One sun he said to his wife, "I am going far this time."

She replied, complaining, "You always leave me! I am going with you!"

The warrior did not want this. He told her, "No! It is too dangerous! I know how to get away from the enemy. I understand what to do."

But the woman coaxed, "You are my husband. They might kill you! If they kill both of us, well, I do not care. I want to go with you!"

The woman got the best of him in their talk, and he finally said, "You can go! But I sometimes go several suns without any food. I travel long ways on foot."

They started and went for many days towards the sunrise. They reached the Big Mountains [Rockies]. It happened that another man, a warrior of a similar powerful *Tah*, was coming from the other side of the mountain, coming in the sunset. He was hunting from a different tribe of Indians. The warrior going towards the sunrise saw a low place in the mountains and directed towards it. The sunset-traveling warrior did the same thing. Both happened to aim for the same low place.

Reaching near the top, they saw each other. Drawing near each other, they talked in sign language. Each told what he was doing, why he was there. The sunrising traveling hunter said, "I am going towards the sunrise. Anybody that I meet, I have to kill him."

The other warrior signaled back, "I am traveling towards the sunset. Anybody that I meet, I must kill."

Then they fought. The woman stood and watched them. She sized up the strange man. She thought, "He is a better man than my husband! If he kills my husband, I will go with him."

But her husband was powerful. Nothing had ever got the best of him. She saw her husband getting the best of the strange warrior. She joined to help this other man. She caught her husband's leg. The fight went on, as she hung onto him. He called to her, "No! You are holding wrong. You have my leg. He will kill me!"

The woman did not let go. The ground was all torn up. It was marked so deeply as to show long afterwards. The woman held on, and finally the man tired out. The strange warrior had the best of him. He got the husband down and killed him. He cut him to pieces, cut off his head, his arms, and his legs. He left him dead, all cut to pieces. He took something to show what he had done in battle. The winner had many followers in his calling because of his strength.

The dead warrior was not well-known for great deeds. It was sometime in the day when he was killed. He lay there all night alone. His wife had gone with the strange warrior. Daylight came, and the dead man heard his *Tah* calling him, "This is not the way I told you! We have given you our power. From all the different animals and birds, you have power. You are not dead."

The man had such powers as he heard, the leading one that of the buffalo. Waking up he heard all the different *Tah* powers, animals on the ground, birds in the trees. Coming to life, he felt around [with his thoughts]. He could not find his head at first. Then he found his head and got himself together as well as he was before the fight, all this by the powers he possessed, given by [through] the animals and the birds. He said to himself, "The only thing I can do is go home. I will go tell my people I nearly got killed. Before I follow him, I will go to my people and tell how I was cut to pieces in the fight, not right away but only for my wife. If not for her, I would not have been killed.

Then the warrior traveled back to his people. When he reached the village, he called his followers together and told them, "I want you to hear what I tell you! It was a hard battle on the mountain. I would not have been killed had not my wife dragged on my leg."

Relatives of his wife said, "We do not believe you! Maybe you killed your wife!"

The returned warrior replied, "No! I want you to go with me. I will show you where we fought, where I lay killed. But I have a strong power!"

Then they went with him. They wanted to see the proof of what he had done. He showed them where the ground was torn up, where deeply marked, where he had lain, all of the different parts. There were the tracks of the woman showing she had gone with the other warrior. Then the people all returned home, for their leader said to them, "I do not want anybody to go with me! I will follow and see where they go. If killed, I will die alone."

The people replied, "All right! We will go and leave you!"

So he followed, trailing the enemy and his own wife for several suns. He came to a village. He thought to wait till night. Then he would look among the teepees. Darkness came, and he began walking through the tepees. He watched how the people were dressed. He fixed himself to look like them, having the same kind of buffalo robe and buckskin. He came in among them. They could not tell he was a stranger. He sized everything up, located the headmen, where the Chief lived near the center of the village. He stood near the Chief's teepee. He began to know, to understand the place. He walked around for a time. A woman came out of the main teepee. Passing close, he recognized his wife. He saw her moving away from the teepee, off some distance. He overtook her and spoke, "I am hunting you! I have found you this night. I came after you! Your relations thought I killed you."

The woman thought, "My husband must be powerful! He was cut all to pieces and is now well." Then she answered him, "You stay here. I cannot go with you just now. I have something in the teepee I am taking with me."

The woman then returned to the tepee. She told the other man she was living with about her husband. She said, "That man was killed. You know how you cut him up! He has changed to become alive. He is now standing outside. Make up your mind how you can kill him. I made arrangements to come to him again. You get several to help you. I will go get hold of him and halloo. Then you hurry and take hold of him."

The Chief got other men, and the woman went outside. She reached her husband and began to talk, "I have been lonesome for you all the time. But I could not help it! I had to come with him."

Her husband thought and then said to her, "If you are going with me, all right! We better go now!"

But the woman argued about it. She told him, "No one has seen you! Nobody sees you! No use to hurry! Let us take a rest before going."

The man thought differently. He replied, "No! We better go!"

The woman continued to coax, "No! I have been lonesome for you! We must sit down here first."

The man thought maybe so. They must sit down close together. She caught him around the neck and held him fast. She hallooed! The men ran out, all of them, tied him tight and fast. They kept him there, lots of the men watching him all night. Morning came and the Chief endured.

"Take down all the tepees. Tepee poles must be piled in one heap. We are moving to another place."

All the people worked, laying the poles in one big pile. All was ready to go. One very old woman was among them, taken as a little girl from the warrior-prisoner's own country. Growing old there, she had a son and a daughter and grandchildren. The prisoner might be a relation from some place. The Chief ordered that the old woman be left there. She could not walk, could not be carried without too much trouble. Her children had to leave her as ordered. They fixed a small tepee for her, left pieces of robes and a little food. If the moving was not too far away, more food would be brought for her. She must stay there as commanded till she died.

The Chief ordered the prisoner carried to the tip of the ricked poles. He said to his followers, "We will burn him to death, put fire all around him and watch him till he burns up. He is not to escape this time."

Fire was placed on all sides of the pole-heap. The poles soon burned fast; the flames reached him. The prisoner said nothing. They watched until the pile burned down, only hot coals remaining. All burned to nothing. The people left, traveling to some new village site. Only the hot coals were glowing there; the man had burned as they went away. These embers soon turned to ashes. By the next morning, nothing seemed left of the burned prisoner.

The sun came up, and the old abandoned woman awoke from sleep. She felt sorry for what had been done. She said to herself, "This man coming so far from towards the sunset must have been my relation. I may have been brought from where he came, my country. Yes, he must have been my relation. I am going to where he was burned. If I can find bones in the ashes, even charred, I will bury them!"

She cried as she hunted through the ashes. She found one piece of bone either from the knee or hip. It was round, as from a joint. No others were in all the ashes. She dug a small hole and lay the bone in the hole. She placed a buffalo robe over the spot. She did not know that the buffalo was his main or leading *Tah* power.

There the bone lay one night. Near morning, she heard a terrible noise where she had buried the bone. Daylight came and, looking, she understood. All the *Tahs* of the burned warrior were there at the burial spot. All of his flying birds, of his ground animals, *Tahs* big and small had gathered at the grave. All were singing *Tah* powers. That warrior under the buffalo robe became live. If the robe had not shaded all around, completely covered the grave, he never would have revived. Perfectly shaded he came to life as a buffalo, with help from other animals and birds. Alive, the warrior raised up, pushing the buffalo robe aside. He looked around. Everybody had left. Tepees were gone; the poles burned.

Walking around, he found the woman at her small tepee. He spoke to her. Sure enough he spoke to her in her own language. She gave him a little food, as she had. He ate it as they talked. She told him the number of her own children and grandchildren, her own people. He instructed her, "You follow the tracks they have made. Travel as you can. If it takes you sometime, you catch up with them. Have people set their tepees all at one side. You know how he killed me. I will kill him the same way! It will be my time, maybe at the next village. I am going home to tell about my wife. She did it against me! I may bring help, for I died because the Chief had help. If any want to come to see where I was killed, they can come.

"Now go! Make yourself strong as you can for the traveling. Have the tepees of your own people set apart as I tell you. I will know when I come! If this is not done, I might kill them too. This time I shall kill him!" The old lady traveled. She grew stronger as she traveled. She was advised [aided] by his strength.

The warrior returned to his own country. He told what had happened, what his wife had done to him. Her brothers and cousins became mad at her. He told how she hung to his neck, and how he could not fight. He told how he was burned, how if no bone had been left in the ashes, he could not have returned to life. He said, "The old woman is now at the new village. Her sons, her daughters and grandchildren are all in a tepee off to one side. If any of you want to go with me, all right! I am going, and I am killing him this time."

A few men, maybe ten, got ready and went with him. They traveled and traveled. He came and showed them where he was burned and killed. From there they followed on the trail several suns. They found the village. Counseling, they thought to wait for the night. The main thing was to first find how the enemy was dressed. They dressed themselves the same way.

Night drew on, and they entered the village, one by one. They did not go in a bunch. Always, someone was watching for the enemy. Advised how to get set, they saw a woman come from the Chief's tepee. Her brothers had said, "If she is found, tie her down! She must die this time!"

Her husband came to her and said, "I have come back again. What do you think about it?"

The woman thought she better go peacefully. She answered, "I will go with you, yes!"

Her husband made reply, "No! I do not want you. I will kill you! I shall kill your man! Powerful, he killed me twice. He will get the same treatment from me this time."

The woman again answered, "No! We better go back home."

Her brothers said to her, "We will tie you down. When that other man is killed, you die with him."

They tied the woman down. Fighting began, hard fighting. The leader had instructed his men not to bother the tepees bunched apart. The old woman had instructed her people not to go outside their tepee. All would be killed not remaining inside. The Chief, the woman's man, was caught. His warriors came to help him. The enemy leaders hurled them ahead. Powerfully he snatched their arms and their legs. Any place he caught them he tore away. Some were killed outright. The Chief was tied down and kept with the woman.

Next morning some of the enemy were still alive, arms torn off, legs missing. Others joined the strange Chief and his band. These were the old woman's people. The prisoner Chief said, "I killed you twice. You are more powerful than I. I do not want to die! I will live under you. You will be the Chief."

The strange Chief answered, "No! I will do to you as you did to me! If you can then come back to life, we will live together."

Then they tore down all the tepees. Piling the poles in one big heap, they burned the man and woman together. They never came back to life. The relations of the woman did not want her. She had gone wrong. They brought the old woman and her relations back with them to her old home. The brave Chief was now looked upon as the greatest of his tribe.

4B. *TAHMAHNAWIS* POWER

Collected April 1921, Informant Unknown

A band of Umatilla hunters were in camp. A great eagle was soaring, circled and soared overhead, far up in the skies. An aged *Tahmahnawis* man was challenged to bring down the eagle with his *Tah*.

He said: "I can do that." The old hunter "shot" his *Tahmahnawis* at the bird, but to no purpose. The eagle continued soaring.

It was then that a younger man said: "You are too old. You cannot kill the eagle with your *Tahmahnawis* power. I will now kill the eagle with my power."

Suiting action to his words, the young man "shot" his *tahmahnawis* at the eagle which immediately came tumbling down through the air, falling dead near the camp. The aged Indian made no comment. He had been beaten by his younger companion.

5. A LEGEND OF DEEP LAKE, THE GRAND COULEE

A young man from Snake River married an Okanogan girl. He was with her and her parents in the root-digging season at Grand Coulee. He had bow and arrows and hunted every day. Sometimes he brought home a rabbit, maybe an occasional bird, but ofttimes nothing; and food was scarce. His young wife told him not to go in a certain direction, that it was bad to go in that direction.

For several days he did not go, minded her, what she told him. But he could find no more rabbits and began to wonder why his wife did not want him to go in that particular direction. Finally he said to himself that he was going to see why she told him that. So without saying anything about it, he went that way; and after a while he came to the great cliff. Looking down, he saw the water.

He thought, "I will go down there and see what is there." He got down the cliff somewhere and sat down on a rock at the edge of the water. He looked down through the clear water and saw lots of fish. He thought, "This is why I was told not to come in this direction. Here are lots of fish, and I will catch some and take them to the lodge. We are starving, and here are plenty of fish. I will take some of them to my people."

He cut an elderberry pole, trimmed a hook on it, and going to the sloping rock again, he began hooking out the fish, the small ones. He soon said, "I do not want these small fish. I will catch a big one." He looked for the biggest salmon and soon got him hooked. The fish was too much for him and pulled him into the lake. Down he went, and that was the last of him. He was never seen again.

He did not return home. The people looked for him all around. Days went by and finally they went down to the lake. There they found his bow and case of arrows, the fish he had caught, lying on the rock all dried up. But no trace of him could be found. Days and moons everybody searched, and each year while digging roots they hunted. Never was he found.

No Indian would go near that lake. It was some monster in it that took the man.[66]

6. THE DWARF MOUNTAIN PEOPLE

Three brothers, *Cee-wal-tis-cou-cou*, *Tem-mot Cio-soota-cots*, and *We-yow Yets-chit-con*, were hunting in the Blue Mountains where there was snow. *Cee-wal-tis-cou-cou*, a tribal warrior and whose widow and daughter are still living (1927), was riding alone. He saw a fresh deer track and proceeded to follow it. Then he noticed a moccasin track which appeared following the deer, not larger than that of a baby's footprint. He could not understand but thought, "Maybe he is also tracking the deer."

After a time, looking a short distance ahead, he saw an old man, an old man not larger than a papoose, dressed in spotted fawn-skin, standing on a log. He had a bow and arrows in a fawn-skin case. Riding up close, *Cee-wal-tis-cou-cou* saw that the little fellow was very old, face wrinkled, eyes set deep in his head. He thought to take *It* home with him. He spoke, but there was no answer. He then motioned for *It* to get on the horse behind him. *It* held out a very oldish-looking hand, and when grasped by *Cee-wal-tis-cou-cou,* leaped to the seat on the horse. *Cee-wal-tis-cou-cou* gathered *It* close and secure in the folds of his blanket, held fast as does the mother riding with her baby so wrapped behind her.

Riding thus, *Cee-wal-tis-cou-cou* met his two brothers. They all counseled and thought to take *It* home with them, to see what *It* would do, what would come of *It*, letting the people see the little old man. They rode on and, although it was daylight and the sun was shining, soon they missed *It* from the blanket held fast and close by *Cee-wal-tis-cou-cou.* None knew when *It* disappeared, or how gone. Nothing was seen of the little old man. Nobody knew where these people live but suppose it is in caves in the rocks. They may have fire. No one knows.

If you are lost in the woods, and hear a calling, do not answer. It is the Little People,[67] and they will take you wrong. It is dangerous to answer unknown callings when in the mountain forests.[68]

PLATE 17: *Pio Pio-maks maks*, Walla Walla chieftain. Edw. S. Curtis photo, c. 1905.

PLATE 18: Chief *Umapine*, Cayuse-Umatilla Indian.
Joseph K. Dixon photo, 1913.

PLATE 19: White Bull, Umatilla Indian. Edw. S. Curtis photo, c. 1910.

PLATE 20: Paul Showaway, Umatilla Indian in ceremonial dress. Frank LaRoche photo c. 1890-1910.

PART FOUR

THE *WATLALA* OR CASCADES INDIANS

I. INTRODUCTORY NOTES

The Cascades or *Watlala* Indians[69] formerly dwelt along the banks of the Columbia River from below modern Hood River (Dog River), Oregon, westward past the Sandy River, the Washougal River, to the vicinity of the mouth of the Willamette River, at Portland, Oregon. The Indians fished for salmon especially at the "cascades" or lower rapids of the Columbia River now submerged in the lake and raised river behind Bonneville Dam. But the *Watlala* also likely fished such rivers as the Sandy River, near Sandy, Oregon, or the Washougal River, near Washougal, Washington, both of which were likely spawning areas for salmon, providing further opportunities for netting or otherwise taking salmon or other fish.

The physiographic details of their immediate surroundings are marked not only by the rapids-choked Columbia River, but by the steep walls of the Cascades Mountains which rise up from the river, and are covered with thick forests of Douglas fir or other conifers. From the moist air currents from the Japanese current and the Pacific Ocean, the mountains receive many inches of rainfall per year, and especially heavy snowfalls in winter.

The *Watlala* had no detailed, scientific study made of their lifeways and culture during the tribe's separate existence during the nineteenth century. Indeed, the tribe was not a large one. In 1805-06 Lewis and Clark estimated their population at 2,800. By 1854, and perhaps as a result of an influenza epidemic(s) of 1829, their population was reported to be 80. Then, after the 1855 treaties with the region's Indians, the *Watlala* were placed onto the Warm Springs Indian Reservation where they lived alongside especially the Wasco, but also the Tenino, Tygh, even some Paiutes, etc. They were not subsequently enumerated separately.

A brief discussion of Cascades Villages, their names and locations, is given in Spier, *Wishram Ethnography*, p. 167-168, and is recalled again here.

"The villages of the Cascades[70] Indians were separated by an interval from the lowest of the White Salmon [Klickitat?] villages. The first location mentioned for them, *wala' la*, was some ten miles below Wind River, which would place it near the "cascades" of the Columbia. There must have been other settlements about the "cascades" of which we do not know. All mentioned below, like all the foregoing, were on the Washington side of the Columbia.

1. *wala' la*, now Slide (?), is doubtfully a village. The word means "lake" (?) and gives its name to the Cascades people, *wala' lidE' lxam.*[71]

2. *sk!Ema'niak* held a population of the Cascades. It was a little below *wala'la* and is indicated on the map near the present town of Skamania.

3. *lxaxwa'lukl* was perhaps two miles below *sk!Ema'niak.* It had a population of 1,000 (?). The name means "they are running by her continually."

4. *nimicxa'ya* was a Cascades village about half a mile below a high rock (*ik!a'lamat*) now known as Castle Rock and about two miles above Cape Horn. (These are not to be confused with the Castle Rock and Cape Horn on the lower Columbia). The population was in the neighborhood of 400."[72]

Little or nothing is available which in extent, detail, or accuracy describes the artifacts and sociofacts of the Cascades Indians. And more's the pity, for such cultural data would both help explain circumstances and help substantiate details of the oral traditional literature of the Cascades or *Watlala* Indians which follows. We have only the scantest hope that this dearth of important detail can at this late date be remedied about a tribal group which resided and fished perhaps on both sides of the Columbia River over a distance of some 70 miles.

But as we pass through time still farther from that era when Native American fishers and hunters peopled the Columbia River's banks, as well pass farther from that time when the Columbia River raged naturally through the several immense systems of rapids or dalles between Vancouver and Wishram, Washington, our need only grows for accurate detailed sources of possible cultural details about these peoples. One possibility from which, we presume, very considerable parallel cultural data might be drawn would be Spier and Sapir, *Wishram Ethnography*, cited in the bibliography hereafter.

PLATE 21: *Kama'gwaih*, Cascade Indian. Edw. S. Curtis photo, c. 1910.

PLATE 22: At the site of the *Wahl' lala* [Cascade] Indians (a Chinookan village). Edw. S. Curtis photo, c. 1910.

PLATE 23: *Wah' lala* bone carving [Cascades Indians].
Edw. S. Curtis photo, c. 1909.

II. TALES OF THE WATLALA INDIANS

7. BATTLE OF THE *AT-TE-YI-YI* AND *TO-QEE-NUT*

In that day the Wolves (*Lal-a-wish*) were five brothers. They talked against *To-qee-nut*, Chief of the Salmon, Chief of all Fishes. The Chinook Salmon (*Qee-nut*) talked against the Wolves. The Wolves prepared to fight the Salmon. Coyote (*Speel-yi*) was a great Chief. He said, "I cannot stop the people from fighting, but I will be there too. I will fight for the Wolves." So the news went to all the people that the Wolves would fight against the Salmon people, fight the Chinook people.

There came the *At-te-yi-yi*, the five brothers, the icy, the strong cold Northeast Winds before whom none could stand.[73] These five brothers said, "All right! We will be there to fight for the Wolves."

So they got together, the five Wolves and the five Wind Brothers. They talked this way, "What will we do with the Salmon?"

The Wind Brothers said, "We think this way. We will wrestle with the Salmon. If we throw him down, ice will be all over the *n-Che-wana*. Ice and cold will be over all the water, cold everywhere."

The Wolves said, "All right! When you throw him down, we will fight and kill all his children. None will be left."

They sent word to the Salmon, "You come! Bring all your children and have a big time on the ice of the *n-Che-wana*. Bring all your people."

To-qee-nut, the Salmon Chief, said, "I cannot help this, my people. I cannot refuse this fight. We will all go, my people. We will all go to meet this boaster."

So all the people went, lined up on each side to fight or wrestle. The Wolves spoke, "All ready for the big trial of strength? *To-qee-nut*, you wrestle with oldest Wind Brother. Wrestle with him first."

To-qee-nut went to wrestle with the oldest Wind, who was not strong. *To-qee-nut* said to his wife and children, "I am afraid! I am afraid of the Winds. Be careful! If you see they are going to beat us, you run away. Run quick and hide."

Both sides were looking on, watching to see the great wrestling match. The Wolves called, "Now ready! Now go!"

The big man of the Salmon and the oldest brother of the Wind, both stripped for wrestling, walked out on the ice, out on the *n-Che-wana*, all covered with ice. The Wind could stand on the ice, but *To-qee-nut* could not stand. They went out a short distance, out on the ice. All the people were looking at the big men wrestling. *To-qee-nut* threw Wind down. Always the oldest brother was not strong. *To-qee-nut* threw Wind down, and from the Salmon side came the victory cry, "*Ow-ow-ow-ow-ow-ow-ow-ow-o-oo*!" The Wind Brothers said nothing. They could not say anything. They kept still.

Then the second Wind Brother stepped out on the ice to wrestle with *To-qee-nut*. He was a little stronger than his older brother, but *To-qee-nut* threw him. Then his people again set up the long shout of triumph. The Wind Brothers kept still. They could not say anything. But all the time *To-qee-nut* kept thinking, "I will die! I will die! They are five against one. They are too many for me. I will die! The Wind Brothers are too strong for me."

Then the third Wind Brother stepped forth to wrestle with *To-qee-nut*. He was a little stronger than either of the older brothers. He stood strong on the ice and threw *To-qee-nut* down hard, threw him quickly. He was dragged and killed on the shore of the frozen *n-Che-wana*. The Wind Brothers yelled, "*Ow-ow-ow-ow-ow-ow-ow-ow-o-oo*!"

Then the five Wolves ran against all the young Salmon, all the young children. There were lots of Wolves, Coyotes and Foxes. All fought the Salmon people. They had first killed the Chief, *To-qee-nut*, then his wife. She had lots of Salmon eggs, eggs in her belly. They threw her down, burst her open. The eggs spilled out. It was on a flat rock; the eggs were scattered all about. All the Salmon people were killed, children and all. The Wind Brothers and all the people on their side now set up [yelled], "*Ow-ow-ow-ow-ow-ow-ow-ow-o-oo*!" The *Qee-nut* are no more! We will now all the time have it cold. Ice will be all over the *n-Che-wana*, cold all the time, ice.

All the Wind side yelled that it would be cold, not warm. Coyote thought, "I did wrong helping the Wolves. They killed a good man, a good people."

The Wolves called loudly to their people, to their side, "Come! Help kill the eggs on the rocks! We do not want one left to grow."

They came and scattered the eggs, destroyed them. That time Coyote stood away back, far back. Coyote did not help destroy the eggs. He said, "We killed a good man, a good Chief! I am sorry!"

He talked that way. Coyote was sorry. He nearly cried. The Wolves yelled loudly, "We have killed all, killed all the Salmon! We have done a great work! Now it will be cold all the time."

The rock where *Top-qee-nut's* wife was killed was cracked deep. The eggs were there, lots of eggs. One egg was deep down. One Wolf called, "One egg, I cannot get it. It is too deep in the rock."

Other Wolves came and tried to lick the egg from the crevice. They licked once, twice, once, twice! They could not get it. They said, "If we don't get it, it will come to life. There will be other Salmon grow up."

The Wolves all tried to lick the egg from the rock, but they failed. All stood with their front feet in the same place, making but two tracks. These tracks can be seen to this day, there in the rock where they stood. It is near the Tumwater, on the Washington side of the *n-Che-wana*, at Wishom.[74] Finally they gave it up. They said, "Let it go. It is dry; it is dead now. It will not grow." They quit. All gave the long, "*Ow-ow-ow-ow-ow-ow-ow-ow-o-oo*!" They had killed all the Salmon, all fishes, and it would now be cold all the time. The five brothers, the Wolves, went to the mountains. They said, "We quit now."

The five Wind Brothers stayed on the *n-Che-wana*, had a cave where they stayed. It was a rock cave at *Wah-pe-us*[75] and was cold, cold and icy. They talked, talked together. "We killed him now! We killed the Salmon! We killed him! His wife and all his children are dead, killed by the Wolves. It will now be cold all the time. It was our work, our big work to do this."

All the Wind people went off the next day, left that place. Clouds came up, came up fast. The clouds grew darker and darker. It rained, rained, and the Spirit which rules helped the one Salmon egg. The egg began to swell. It rained; water went there where the egg was in the split rock. Clouds stayed, and it rained, rained more and more. The egg swelled bigger, still bigger. The Spirit still helped, helped that egg to come to life. It rained five days and five nights, when a little fish came out from that egg. On the sixth day it went into the river, went with the water from the rock. The little fish grew. It went down to the mouth of the *n-Che-wana*, near the ocean. At the mouth of the *n-Che-wana*, it found its grandmother, an old woman. From a little Salmon he grew and found his grandmother, found her far down where the *n-Che-wana* enters the ocean.

The grandmother knew from away off, knew from where she was, that her son had been killed by the Wind Brothers, thrown on the ice and killed by the Wolves. She told the little boy, "My son, your father was killed, killed by the Wind Brothers. His wife and all his children were killed, all but you. I knew it before you came. I am glad, glad that you have come, my little grandchild. I am glad you have come back."

The grandmother caressed her little grand-child, talking to him all the time, telling him how glad she was to see him. She knew, knew when the fight was going on, although she was far away and near the sea. The little Salmon boy said, "Tell me how my father was killed. Yes, tell me how I saved myself alone, how I am alive today."

She told him all, knew all and told it to him. Then she worked to make the boy grow, to make him grow fast and strong. She had Indian medicine to rub on him. She made him bathe every morning. It was to make him grow, to make him strong. She said, "You prepare! Bathe in cold water all winter. Practice! Try your strength, grow strong, and in the spring go fight the Wind Brothers. I am going to fix it, fix five baskets of oil, salmon oil for your feet to stand strong on the ice.[76] There are five brothers of the Wind against my grandchild. I will help you to stand strong before them."

All winter the boy bathed in cold water, bathed, took hard exercise all winter. When spring came, he was big! Tall! Strong! His grandmother said to him, told him often, "I am glad, my grandchild! I am glad! You will be strong, stronger than my son, your father. You will not fall before the Winds."

Early spring came. The boy went outside the tepee. He looked around, all around. He said to his grandmother, "Now look at me!"

She had a small mat lodge, lived there. She went out to look at him. She watched him to see what he would do. He was big, tall, strong. He went a short distance to a thicket and pulled up small trees, pulled them easily and threw them on the ground. His grandmother was glad, glad that he was so strong. She said, "That is right, my grandchild! You will be strong enough in two moons more."

That is the way the Indians used to be. They did those things to make them strong in the hunt, strong in the battle. The boy twisted trees the size of his arm, twisted them to their roots. He would say, "Look at me! See how strong I am, how I can twist and pull up trees."

The grandmother was pleased. She would watch her grandchild and say, "Yes! You are strong my grandchild. You are now stronger than was your father. You will not fall before the Winds."

These things he did for five days; then he pulled up trees that fifty men could not shake. The grandmother said, "That is right! You will beat those people, the boastful Winds. You will not be thrown, will not be killed by them like your father."

The boy was now stronger than ever. He went outside and said, "Look at me! See what I will now do, my grandmother."

There were big rocks lying around. One was bigger than the others, a great rock like a tepee, like the mat lodges of the people who are gone. He walked to that rock, picked it up. He threw it to the middle of the *n-Che-wana*. He threw it easily; it was not hard for him to throw it. The old grandmother was glad, glad that her grandchild was so strong. She said, "Oh, my grandchild! You are strong! You are brave! The Winds, the cold, bad people cannot stand before you. You will beat them. You will not fall before them. I will help you; I will give you the five baskets of oil for your feet."

In this way *We-now-y-yi*, the son of *To-qee-nut*, grew up; this way he prepared himself to fight the cold Winds.[77] He said, "I will fix it; I will fix it about this boastful Wind."

The old woman was sorry because her first son had been killed. She cried, but she was now glad that her grandchild was so strong. He would stand and fight the Wind Brothers, stand on the ice at *Weh-pe-us*, on the *n-Che-wana*.

For six moons did *We-now-y-yi* prepare for the battle, for six moons, until salmon would run in the spring. Every day he practiced at everything: lifting to get strong feet; throwing to get strong arms; running, jumping to get strong legs; pulling up trees to get a strong back, strong shoulders. He thought to get a strong mind, strong head. He said to his grandmother, "They cannot beat me! The Winds cannot stand before me. Five days more and I will go fight the five brothers, the Winds. Get ready the five baskets of oil."

The grandmother answered, "Yes, my grandchild, I will fix the five baskets of oil for you, for your feet to stand strong on the ice. You will not fall."

The Winds had a slave woman, a sister to the old grandmother.[78] They watched her closely, would not let her go anywhere. They treated her badly. The Winds had a sister, *Ats-te-yi-yi*, a cripple, a sister to the Chief Wind. Every morning this *Ats-te-yi-yi* would go out, then come and befoul the old slave woman's hair. It was all bad. The grandmother told *We-now-y-yi* all about this, how her sister was nearly starved with no food, no robes. Cold all the time with icicles hanging to her hair, she was nearly dead.

We-now-y-yi finished the five days. He finished practicing, finished preparing for the battle. "Good-bye, my grandmother. I am now going to meet the Wind Brothers on the ice of the *n-Che-wana*. I will kill the Winds, the five brothers who killed my father. Good-bye! I will go now."

The grandmother put her arms around him, caressed him. She said, "All right! Go! Be strong before the Winds. Take these five baskets of oil. When you get to my sister, she will tell you all about this oil, how to use it. She knows and will fix it for you. Go! Good-bye, my grandchild. You will not fall before the Winds. You will beat them on the ice, beat them in the wrestling match."

We-now-y-yi answered, "All right!"

We-now-y-yi came on foot. He came to the Cascades. There he threw trees, threw rocks far out into the river. He pulled up big trees, threw them into the *n-Che-wana*. He tore big rocks from the ground, hurled them far out into the water. He felt strong. He practiced his strength on everything, in every way as he came. He kept saying, "Nothing can beat me! Nothing can stand before me. I am *We-now-y-yi*, the *To-qee-nut's* son. I am stronger than was my father. The Winds, the five brothers, the cold Winds cannot stand before my breath. I will beat them! I will throw them on the ice of the *n-Che-wana*. I will kill this cold. It cannot stay everywhere all the time."

Thus *We-now-y-yi* traveled up the *n-Che-wana*. He came close to Celilo, where the Winds lived in the rock cave. The *n-Che-wana* was covered with ice, cold all the time. Salmon was the warm wind, the Chinook wind. *We-now-y-yi* was his son. He got close to the Winds. He thought, "These people will know that I am coming."

Thoughts, like breath, go ahead. The old aunt, covered with ice, cold, starving, sat in her little mat lodge. The breath of *We-now-y-yi* broke the icicles in her hair. They fell to the ground. She groaned, "*Ah-h-n-nn*! He is coming back." She knew all. Then *We-now-y-yi* walked slowly. He saw the little mat hut, this side of the Winds' cave-house. He went in. She could only whisper, "I am poorly! They are treating me badly! Every morning the sister of the Winds comes and filths my hair. Every morning you will hear a noise at the door. It is her. She comes but does not look at me."

We-now-y-yi answered, "All right! I will fix her! I feel sorry they make a slave of you. Go out and cut a rosebush with thorns. Tomorrow I will fix this girl, this lame sister of the Winds."

The old aunt went out and brought back the rosebush with all its thorns. Then they slept a little. In the morning they got up. The aunt said, "Sit near the door; hide your rosebush near the door. She will come. She will not look around; she will not see you."

We-now-y-yi sat by the door. Soon he heard a noise coming. Yes! It was *Ats-te-yi-yi*! She came in! She did not look around, did not look at the old woman. When she backed near the old aunt, *We-now-y-yi* struck her on the naked [buttocks?] with the thorny rosebush, struck her hard. *Ats-te-yi-yi* cried, "*Owo*!"

Ats-te-yi-yi ran out of the house, blood running down her legs. She hurried back to her brothers, the Winds, and said, "Our enemy has come to life. I do not know how he is alive, but he is there in the mat-lodge with the old woman. I do not think that the old woman did this to me! I do not think that she struck me with the rosebush thorns."

Ats-te-yi-yi told her brothers this, how she had been struck. They answered, "Yes! Last night we were a little afraid. Last night the warm wind came a little, and we were afraid. It is he! It is Salmon come to life again. He has come to meet us on the ice, to wrestle with us on the ice of the *n-Che-wana*."

Then the Wind Brothers sent word to all the people, to everybody to come and see the great wrestling match, see it again that day. The five Wolves came from the mountains. The big chiefs came, all the chiefs of the Foxes, the Birds, all came bringing their people. Word was sent out, "Salmon has grown up! Salmon wants to wrestle, has come to wrestle with the Winds."

We-now-y-yi had his five baskets of oil. The old aunt fixed them, made everything ready. That meant five baskets of oil against the five Wind Brothers and against the five Wolves. The old woman put oil on his feet, on the feet of *We-now-y-yi*, the strong. The Winds saw him. They called to him friendly, "Is that you, our friend? Have you come to wrestle with us?"

We-now-y-yi made answer the same way, "Yes! I have come to do this thing. I have come to wrestle with you, my friends, wrestle on the ice of the *n-Che-wana*."

The Winds thought, "He is only one; he is not strong. We are five; we are strong. We will kill him, this boasting Salmon."

It was near mid-sun. All went to see the wrestling, went near the bank of the *n-Che-wana*, all covered with ice, ice made by the winds. The five Wind Brothers laughed at *We-now-y-yi*, laughed long! *We-now-y-yi* answered, "I will be there! I will meet you on the ice of the *n-Che-wana*."

Ats-te-yi-yi, the lame sister, was there. The people all wanted to see. Coyote, the big Chief said, "I am glad that my grandson is here to fight the Winds. I will help him."

Both *We-now-y-yi* and the old woman went out. She had the five baskets of oil. All the people looked at him. See! He was a big man—strong, strong arms! Strong legs! Strong all over! Strong head and strong heart. Coyote looked at him, sized him up. Coyote said, "Yes! We will win! We will beat the Wind Brothers. *We-now-y-yi* is stronger than was his father. He will stand strong to wrestle."

All five of the Wind Brothers were to wrestle against *We-now-y-yi*, the Salmon. He said to his aunt, the old woman, "Soon as I get to the place on the ice, pour one basket of oil at my feet. Pour it on the ice at my feet."

She answered him, "All right! I will pour the oil. It will make you stand strong."

We-now-y-yi stood in his place. The old aunt poured the oil at his feet, poured it on his feet, on the ice. All the people were looking at him. All the people were anxious to see him. He looked big, looked strong, all stripped on the ice for wrestling. The Wolves were a little afraid. The oldest brother, the oldest Wind, stepped out to wrestle with *We-now-y-yi*. He was not so strong-looking. They tried strength four times, when Wind was thrown on the ice, killed. His head was cut, burst on the ice. Coyote gave a long "*Ow-ow-ow-ow-ow-ow-ow-ow-o-oo*!' It was the cry of the victor. The Wind and their people could not say anything. They had to keep still.

The second brother of the Wind stepped out to wrestle with the Salmon. He was a little stronger. They stood to wrestle, stripped naked on the ice. The old aunt poured oil at the feet of *We-now-y-yi*. All was ready! Right away they wrestled. It was the same way as with the first brother, only a little longer, a little harder struggling. Three times *We-now-y-yi* swung the Wind. Three times they swung and bent hard. Then the fourth time the Wind was whirled, thrown on the ice; his head burst, killed. Coyote again called the long yell of the victor, called it long and loud. The five Wolves stood mad. They said to each other, "They will beat us! Coyote! Coyote, the big Chief is against us."

The third Wind came out to match his skill and strength with that of the mighty *We-now-y-yi*. They stood. The old woman poured the third basket of oil at the feet of Salmon. *We-now-y-yi*, the Salmon, stood strong on the ice. They wrestled. *We-now-y-yi* turned the Wind three times, turned him slowly. Then he whirled him fast, threw him on the ice, bursting his head. The other two Wind brothers were scared. Coyote gave louder the cry of victory. His side called to the Wind Brothers, "Hurry up! Hurry up and wrestle! We cannot stand here so long!"

The fourth brother walked out on the ice. The old aunt came and poured the fourth basket of oil at the feet of *We-now-y-yi*, poured it on the ice at his feet. He stood strong, a big man. They began to wrestle. The Wind was stronger than were any of his three brothers who had been killed. He stood and wrestled strong. Four times he was swung by *We-now-y-yi*, four times slowly swung. Then *We-now-y-yi* whirled him quickly, threw him and his head burst on the ice.

Coyote cried the long call of the victor, of the best man. The last Wind Brother stood afraid. He said to himself over and over, "He will kill me, kill me sure. All my brothers are dead, killed by this Strong Salmon. He will kill me, but I cannot run. It is the law that I must fight, must wrestle and die."

Coyote's side called, "Hurry up! Hurry up! Wrestle with Salmon. Do not be afraid!"

Slowly he came, came slowly out on the ice. He stood where his brothers stood, where all four of his brothers were killed. The last basket of oil was poured by the old aunt at the feet of *We-now-y-yi*. *We-now-y-yi* placed his feet. He said to himself, "I am going to stand strong, this, the last time."

Then they wrestled, wrestled harder, faster. The match was closer than the last two. The last and youngest Wind was strong, struggled hard. Six times did *We-now-y-yi* turn him, six times slowly. Six times he had turned him, then the seventh whirled him fast, threw him on the ice. His head burst like those of his four older brothers. The last of the Wind Brothers lay dead at the feet of *We-now-y-yi*, the son of *To-qee-nut*, Chief of the Chinooks. It was then that *Ats-te-yi-yi*, the lame sister of the Wind, ran crying to the *n-Che-wana*. All were after her to kill her. She went into the water through a hole in the ice. She escaped.[79]

Coyote yelled louder, louder the cry of the strongest side. All the people shouted, were glad. Coyote called, "We beat them! We beat them, those bad peoople. Now it will be warm. We will have nice, rich food. The salmon will come, all the salmon we want to eat. Now we will all stand, all run against the five Wolves."

Coyote said this. He ran against the Wolves, heading all the people fighting against them. The Wolves fled to the Cascade Mountains, are there yet. The Wolves said, "Coyote is Chief! We cannot beat him! We cannot stand before him."

Coyote was then the big Chief; he commanded. He said, "*Ats-te-yi-yi* has escaped into the water. For this reason it will be a little cold, but not as cold as it has been. It cannot remain cold all the time."

The ice at that moment melted in the *n-Che-wana*, ran down to the ocean. There is now only a little ice in the winter, a little ice during a few moons only. This was many thousand snows ago. There is no record, but that is the talk. That time Coyote said to *We-now-y-yi*, the big Salmon Chief, "I am going to foretell. From here, from *Wah-pe-us*, from *Skein*, people will live to the mouth of the *n-Che-wana*, to the ocean. They will be different people, different from all kinds of bird and animal people, and all will eat freely by and by. Nothing will be paid. Food is for all kinds of people, free."

The Salmon Chief said to Coyote, said when they were together, "Yes! You put it down that way, put the law that way. All will be friendly and good. We killed the Wind Brothers. They were strong, but we killed them. These bad people are now dead. We will have no more war at this time."

It was that way. And now from that time, Coyote said, "Other people will come; and when they meet and have a big time, when they play games of any kind, the Coyote call by the victors will be given: '*Ow-ow-ow-ow-ow-ow-ow-ow-o-oo*!' The beaten party must keep still, cannot say anything."

That is the law, given by Coyote at that time. It stands today, in games and in war. That cry is the cry of the victor only.[80,81]

8. ORIGIN OF THE HORSE
Chief Meninock, July 4, 1921

The horse [*Kuc-ci*] came from the East somewhere. It was never found on the ridges and dry land as now. The horse was in the lakes; it lived there.

Once the Indians held a meeting, a council. A lake was there. A young woman went to bring water. She saw an Indian man, who took her. She did not know who he was, but he was a real person. This was early in the fall, and that woman never came back. The Indians hunted for her but never found her. She was lost.

It was the next spring, early spring, when a man went to hunt rabbits and small game. He came to a swamp; some grass and feed were there. He saw a brown stallion in that swamp. The lost woman was there, about one-fourth horse. He saw that she had a mane and tail, and hair on her body. This woman had been the wife of the Chief of the tribe.

The man hurried back to the village. He told what he had seen in the swamp, told the Chief how he had seen his wife and how she appeared. A council was held, and it was decided that they go see what was in the swamp. They did not believe all that the man had told them. They would go see for themselves. They went to the swamp and hid behind some bushes. They saw the brown stallion. They saw the woman, now partly changed to a horse. They now believed what the man had told them. He had spoken true words.

In those days the Indians had deerskin ropes for packing their bedding of skins and furs. They surrounded the swamp with these ropes, where the stallion and the woman were. Two colts were with them. The stallion broke the line and escaped, the two colts following him. The woman was behind and was caught. She was like a wild horse. The two colts turned back, came near their mother. One was about three moons old, the other one moon old. At first the woman did not talk, could not talk. But finally she spoke a few words, then talked more. She told them that she could not help it; she had to go with the stallion. She now had two children and wanted to take care of them. The Chief and his people let her go.

Three months later they saw her again. She was then completely changed to an *iat* [woman] *kuc-ci*. In three snows more there were plenty of *kuc-ci mah*. Every snow after that the Indians caught any horses wanted in the swamps. They would catch a one-snow colt and use it to pack from place to place. One would do a whole family, for all walked. They were afoot in those days. They would pay high for a horse. It was too costly for everyone to own a horse.

The horses kept coming on from the East, brought from the East to the *n-Che-wana*.[82] They are now here in plenty. The Indians always believe that when you hallo, when you call to the horse, he understands you. He stops, or looks up. This is because of the *iat kuc-ci*. They understand our language, for they came from the *iat*.[83]

9. HOW A WATER-BALL WAS MADE

Che-pos To-cos (Owl Child), March 5, 1932

You know the Sweathouse, how it is made — how the rocks are first heated, and then put into the small hole in the ground just inside the doorway; how water must be brought and sprinkled on these hot stones to make a fog for the sweat. Three men had the rocks hot all ready for the sweat. Then they found they had no water-basket to bring water from the lake. They must try their Power to see who could bring the water.

One man took an open-woven [sic] basket, all full of holes, and dipped it into the lake. He brought the basket full of water and set it down at the sweathouse. He had a strong power. Another man took a dip-net — used to catch fish — and, going to the lake, dipped into the water and brought it filled and sat it by the basket that had been filled. The water did not leak out.

The last man must now try his power. He waded into the lake until the water came above his knees. Then he began making a waterball, piling it up and shaping it with his hands. He made a round ball of water, large as a good-sized cooking basket. He lifted it to his shoulder, carried it to the sweathouse, and sat it down by the basket and the dipnet of the other men. The water-ball held its shape, did not melt down. Then the man stuck his finger into it, and the water ran out. It was great work.

You do not know what Power this man possessed? I will tell you. When a small boy, he was sent out somewhere in a lonely place to try to find power from something. The seal came and talked to him. It told him to do as it was telling him, and when he should be grown up he would have this power to handle the water. Inside the fish, inside the seal, is the sack [air bladder] which you can take out. It was given the fish and the seal to help them handle themselves in the water; they blow it up with air. Land animals do not have this, and it was this power given by the seal to the boy when alone in the night darkness. No other man had such power as did this man.[84]

10A. A CASCADE LEGEND

Che-pos To-cos (Owl Child), June 7, 1926

A Chief of the Cascade tribe had a brother. This brother declared that if he died, if he were killed, he would stay dead five days and then return back to life again. The Chief had several wives, one of them fine-looking. He plotted to trap his brother, to see if he was telling the truth about his life if killed. He said to this wife, "Go with my brother some place. Try him! But do nothing. Wait till I can be there afterwards."

The woman did this, but the man refused. He said, "No! I cannot do this. You are my brother's wife."

When the woman reported this to the Chief, he said to her, "Try him again! Keep trying him."

She did so, and finally the brother agreed. But when they were under the blanket, the Chief came and lifted up the blanket. The woman sprang up. The brother looked up and saw his brother with a bow and five arrows. The brother lifted his left arm, covering his eyes with the forepart of his arm. He lay on his side, exposing his heart by lifting his arm. The Chief shot the five arrows deep into his body, piercing his heart. The brother lay dead.

The next day the Chief sent this same wife to see if his brother was still dead. She reported that he was. The next day she again went, and coming back reported the body beginning to swell, turning yellow. The five arrows had been poisoned with the *Wahk-puch* [rattlesnake] spit. The third day she went. The body was swollen worse. Flies were about the body, depositing their worm-eggs. When she reported this to her husband, the Chief cried. He now thought his brother had lied to him. The fourth day he sent his wife, who found the body covered with the fly-worm. The body was still swollen, worms crawling over it.

The fifth day there came an awful storm. Thunder filled the forest; lightning lit up the darkness of the clouds. It was a heavy rain that fell for a long time.

Next morning a voice was heard outside the lodge door, calling them to get up. It was the dead brother. He came inside, and after breakfast he said to the Chief, "Call all the people together." He gave gifts and said to them, "I am now big. I will be bad no more. I will never want anything from others. I will not want the wife of another man. I will not take your women from you. I will not take anything belonging to others. From where the sun shines, I will be a good man."

He became a good man, married, and was useful to his tribe.

10B. A LEGEND OF THE CASCADE TRIBE
Che-pos To-cos (Owl Child), March 5, 1932

There were two brothers among the Cascade Indians. The oldest one was a chief, and had four or five wives. The younger brother was single. The Chief heard this younger brother say: "If I die, it will be five suns that I remain dead, and then come back to life. No difference if I become all swollen up, and maybe worms are on me, if I am ready to burst; I will come back to life again."

The Chief did not believe. He thinks: "What my brother says can not be so. If he is bad wounded, he may live one moon before dying."

He told his best wife to go with his brother, and fool him. She tried, but the young man would not listen; would not go with her. The Chief told her to try again. She did so, and won. The Chief told her to go to the Cascades where there was a big fir tree. He said: "Go to the big tree where I tell you. I will follow you."

The Chief had medicine arrows; five poisoned arrows. If you are only light wounded with one of these, you die. The Chief followed with his five poison-arrows. The young man and woman came to the big tree and lay down. The Chief came up close, standing over the younger brother. The woman drew away. The young man saw some one standing by him, and raised his arm, shading his eyes, looking up to see who it was. While he lay thus, the Chief shot all five of his arrows into the young man's exposed side.

The young brother died, became yellow in death. The Chief and wife covered him with a robe and left him. They went home, and stayed all night in their lodge. Next morning the Chief did not want to see his brother, so sent his wife to go look if he was dead. She came back and said: "He is lying there dead." That day passed, and night came with its sleeping. Next morning the Chief again sent his wife to see if the dead [brother] was still there. She returned and said: "Yes, he is lying dead where we left him."

Another night passed, and the Chief sent his wife to see for the third time if the brother was still there. She returned with the message: "He is there, and beginning to swell up now."

The fourth night came and passed; and the Chief sent his wife again to see if the body was still there. She came back and told him: "He is still there as we left him. I found flies all over his body, and the worms have come in plenty. The body is now ready to burst open."

The fifth morning drew near, but it was still dark. There was heard a great thunder rolling in the skies. The wind blew in a terrible storm, breaking down the biggest trees in the forest. The earth trembled with the rushing wind sweeping over it, howling everywhere. The Chief and his wife lay listening to the wild storm, but went to sleep after it had passed.

The young man had found his life, and came to the Chief's lodge and built a fire. He was wet and cold from the big storm. He called: "You people better get up. I am hungry!"

The Chief heard the voice. It was just like that of his dead brother left at the great tree. He was scared. He would not uncover his head to look; but told his wife: "Look, and see who is here; who is calling."

She looked and told him: "It is your brother!"

They got up, and the wife did cooking. They ate. The younger brother told the Chief: "Tell all the people to come." The Chief did so, but he had never done this before.

The people came, and wondered what it was about. They had a big feast. The young man told them [that] not any must leave until after he had talked. Then he got up and said: "I am not brave. I have not made myself a brave man. I died for five suns; and I will now be good. I will be bad no more. I am good from this sun on."

That was all that he said. The people went home. The boy got married, and was a powerful chief after that time. They did this in olden times. Took the place of other chiefs. This happened among the Cascade Indians; who were once a strong tribe.[85]

11A. THE STRONG BOY OF THE CASCADES

Che-pos To-cos (Owl Child), October 1923

Tos-cas wo-hah[86] was Chief of the Cascades. His village was where the Bridge of the Gods stood over the *n-Che-wana.* A bad man, he had two hundred wives, and he owned a big lodge. Powerful and strong, his feet were half the length of a lodgepole. Every evening he made smooth the sand all about his lodge, smoothed it down, even and level. He did this so he would know if anybody came near his place during the dark. No tracks could be made there without his seeing them.

When any of his wives brought a baby, the Chief would always ask which it was, a boy or girl. If a boy, he killed it. He was afraid the boy would grow up and become stronger than himself. If the baby was a girl, all was well. He let it live. And the Chief kept the sanded ground leveled all the time about his great lodge. Nobody could come without his seeing the tracks.

Ni-ti-it was one of the wives who came from the White Salmon. When her baby first cried, the Chief asked her, "What is the child?" Is it a boy or girl?"

Ni-ti-it was afraid, for her baby was a boy. She answered, "My child is a girl."

Every morning the Chief examined the ground on every side of his lodge to see if tracks had been made during the night. Two snows passed; *Ni-ti-it* kept her baby hid all the time. One sun she said to the Chief, "My child wants to see my people. I want to take her to see my father and mother, to see all my people."

The Chief was willing, and he said, "All right! You can take the child to see your people."

Ni-ti-it was glad. She loaded five canoes with gifts and went traveling on the *n-Che-wana*. She came to the White Salmon, where her father and mother lived. She told them all about everything, told how she had blinded her husband about her baby. She said, "I want him to grow up a big boy, big, strong and powerful! I want to raise him here. I cannot keep him hid much longer."

Ni-ti-it remained with her parents, where she could raise her boy in safety. The bad Chief still kept the sand smoothed and level about his lodge. The boy grew up. His feet were an arrow's length longer than those of the old man, his father. The Boy grew strong, grew powerful with strength. He practiced his strength each sun. From morning till night, he trained to be strong.

Between the White Salmon and the Cascades is a great rock, by the *n-Che-wana*. Larger than a tepee, it stands apart from the cliff, separated by a chasm. The boy placed this rock there. The boy stepped across the deep space and sat on the top of the rock, which is higher than the rest of the cliff. You can see this big rock. It is standing there to this day.

The boy was now big and strong. He went to the bad Chief's lodge while it was dark, and went inside the doorway.[87] Then he returned to his mother's lodge at White Salmon. Daylight came. The old man, going out, saw great moccasin tracks in the leveled sand. He saw where they had entered his doorway, saw where they led away again. He measured the footmarks there in the sand. *Eh*! They were longer than his own! The Chief studied hard, "Who has a larger foot than my own? *Ni-ti-it* lied to me! The baby was not a girl."

The Chief sent three of his best men to bring the boy, sent three strong men, powerful men! They went! When they got to the camp, two stayed in the canoe; the other one went to *Ni-ti-it's* lodge. He entered the doorway and said to the young man, "We want you! Come with us!"

The young man replied, "No! I will not go with you."

The man went back to the canoe and told the two men, "He will not come. We must go up and get him!"

The three strong men now went to the lodge. They said, "We want you!"

The boy was not scared! He was not afraid! He made reply, "No! I will not go with you!"

The three strong men took hold of the boy. They could not handle him! He squeezed their arms in his hands and crushed the bones. He was powerful, was stronger than all three of them! They left him and returned home. They said to the Chief, "We cannot handle him! He squeezed our bones and broke them."

The bad Chief heard this and said to his people, "There will be war! Be ready to fight."

The Chief and his warriors went in a hundred canoes. They had a big fight! The boy, alone, whipped them all. He crushed his father's bones with his hands. The Chief and his warriors returned home to the Cascades.

The next sun the boy started for his father's place. He arrived there and called, "Come out from your lodge, Chief, and fight! It is your son who calls you!"

The Chief was scared! He would not come out from his lodge. The boy entered the doorway, went up close to his father. He took hold of him, handled him easily. He handled him like a cradled papoose. When he got him outside the doorway, he spoke, "You will be Chief no more! I am the one Chief! If you do not say you will not be Chief, I know what I will do with you. I am going to be Chief myself."

The old man asked the boy, "What will you do with me?"

The boy made answer, "I will not tell you! Only myself knows."

The old man then agreed, "All right! I will give up! You can be Chief! Do you take all my lodges?"

The boy answered him, "No! Leave them here where they are."

Thus, was the power of the Bad Chief of the Cascades broken. It was killed by the son whose life was saved in the lie told by his own mother. That lie was good.

11B. A CASCADE INDIAN LEGEND
Che-pos to-cos (Owl Child)

A Cascade Chief had many wives and a big, round lodge. Every morning he would go into the water, bathing. He could walk on it as on the ground. He would only sink in it just a little.

When a child was born, he would ask the mother, his wife, "what is it, boy or girl?" If it was a boy, he killed it. If it was a girl, he let it grow. This was a law he always followed.

He had one woman [wife] from *Nom-i-neet.*[88] Her baby came a boy. The Chief asked her, "What is it?"

The mother wanted to keep her child, and she answered, "It is a girl." She had to lie to save its life.

She kept the baby for several suns, and then told the Chief, "I would like to go to *Nom-i-neet.* I want to show my girl baby to the people there, my own people." In this she lied to the Chief again, telling him when she would return in one moon's time.

So he let her go, and she went for good. She went and stayed, for she was afraid he would kill her baby. The boy grew to be ten snows old. He practiced to become strong. He grew rapidly to manhood. The Chief had long feet, longer than any of the warrior's feet. He kept loose dirt all around his lodge so he could see tracks even of the chipmunk.

When the boy had reached 25 snows, his mother told him all about his father, what he had done, and how he got up mornings and looked to see if anything came to his lodge. That night the boy went to the Chief's home and walked over the soft ground and entered his father's lodge. The next morning the Chief went out and saw tracks a little longer than his own. He thought, "Who can that be? Longer tracks than my own! My wife lied to me! The baby was a boy! It was he who made these tracks."

The Chief then picked two of the strongest men to go bring the boy to the Cascades. He said to them, "If he will not come himself, bring him."

The two strong men went to bring the boy. They found him in his mother's lodge, sitting on a bearskin robe. They told him, "We come to take you to your father." The boy made no reply. They spoke again, "You understand what we say. You better do it! We will take you anyhow!"

They grabbed him, both of them. They could not move him! He cracked the bones in the arms of both men. They went home, arms broken. When they got there, they told the Chief, "We could not bring the boy. He is powerful! We have no arms now!"

The Chief sent more men, lots of canoes. They had no horses. When they got there, the mother had on a ceremonial cap of all colors. If you looked at her cap, you dropped dead. She was a powerful woman. The men were all killed.

The boy then carried a rock that many men together could not carry. He carried it a short distance and sat it down. It can be seen to this day on the bank of the *Neche Wana*[89] between the Cascades and Hood River. It is known as Castle Rock.

INDEX OF MOTIFS

For each oral narrative the *motifs* have been noted hereafter. By *motif* we mean that ". . . smallest element in a tale having a power to persist in tradition. . . . Most motifs fall into three classes. First are the actors in a tale. . . ; second come certain items in the background of the action, magic objects, unusual customs, strange beliefs, and the like; . . . in the third place there are single incidents — and these comprise the great majority of motifs" (Thompson 1946:415.) We have employed Thompson's *Motif-index of folk-literature*, also his *Tales of the North American Indians*.

PART TWO. TALES OF THE TENINO-WARM SPRINGS INDIANS

1. *NASH-LAH*

A. Mythological Motifs

A522.1.3.	Coyote as culture hero
A530.1.1.	Coyote gives people names; cf. A257. How animals received their names
A530.1.1.1.	Coyote assigns names to the animals
A530.1.2.	Coyote assigns attributes to the animals
A530.1.2.1.	Coyote designates eagle as the bravest, best bird; cf. A165.1.2. Eagle as god's bird; also B242.1.1. Eagle, king of the birds
A530.1.2.2.	Coyote designates owl to be a "big medicine man;" cf. B511. Animal as healer
A530.1.2.3.	Coyote designates wolf to be the best hunter; but cf. A2455.1. Wily wolf is a thief; also A165.1.1.1. Wolves as god's dogs
A530.1.2.4.	Coyote designates bear to be the strongest; cf. B746. Bear could formerly lift mountain
A530.1.2.5.	Coyote designates *Qee-nut* to be the "best of all fish" [salmon]
A530.1.2.6.	Coyote designates sturgeon to be the largest river fish
A530.1.2.7.	Coyote designates himself as the wisest, smartest of all animals; but cf. A2525.3. Why fox is sly
A530.1.3.	Coyote assigns attributes [ever after] to *Nash-lah*: to be dangerous, but no longer deadly; cf. B17.2.1. Hostile sea-beasts; also B91.5.2. Lake-serpent (monsters); cf. D2151.4. Magic calming of whirlpool
A535.1.	Culture hero swallowed and escapes from swallowing animal

D. Magic

D902.	Coyote threatens sisters with magic rain (to dissolve dung "sisters")
D908.1.	Coyote finds people inside monster to be cold, starving
D1002	Magic excrements
D1312.1.1.	Excrements as advisors
D1602.	Self-returning magic objects [dung]; cf. D1686. Magic objects(s) depart and return at formulistic command
D1610.6.4.	Speaking excrements

F. Marvels

F811.22.1.	Dry wood and pitch
F819.	Armload of sagebrush (fuel) taken in monster
F836.3.	Extraordinary flint knives (5) — sever heart of swallowing monster; cf. G512.1.1.1. Ogre killed with magic knife(s)
F838.3.	Marvelous flint knives (5)
F882.3.	Extraordinary fire — kindled in belly of monster
F911.3.	Animal (monster) swallows man (not fatally) F911.6. All-swallowing monster
F911.6.1.	All-swallowing monster: takes in people
F912.	Victim kills swallower from within; see also K952. Animal (monster) killed from within
F912.2.	Victim kills swallower from within by cutting
F912.3.2.	Swallowed person cooks and eats portions of swallower's heart
F914.	Swallowed people are disgorged when monster coughs in death throes
F964.6.	Fire made inside monster

G. Ogres

G332.1.	Swallowing monster — [dwells in Columbia River at the tumwater] — swallows people in canoes
G427.	Monster swallows Coyote
G582.2.	River-ogre appeased with food

K. Deceptions

K1771.	Bluffing threat by Coyote — call rain against his "sisters"

L. Reversal of Fortune

L311.6.	Coyote triumphs, overcomes swallowing monster; cf. A531.4. Culture hero conquers sea monster
L434.1.1.	Arrogance of Coyote — as "know-it-all"

M. Ordaining the Future

M161.2.1.	Vow by Coyote to avenge monster's killing of people
M324.1.	Prophecy: coming of the Indian people

P. Society

P672.5.	Taunting monster with insults

S. Unnatural Cruelty

S139.9.	Death to people by monster

Z. Miscellaneous Groups of Motifs

Z71.3.3. Five [5 flint knives][5 sisters]
Z183. "Huckleberries" — euphemism for dung

2. THE *PAH-HO-HO KLAH*

F. Marvels

F451.2.0.7. *Pah-ho-ho Klah* [*Te-chum mah*?] are diminutive, invisible dwarfs living high in the Cascade Mountains
F451.2.1.1.1. *Pah-ho-ho Klah* [*Te-chum mah*] are small, perhaps 18 inches tall
F451.2.7.11 *Pah-ho-ho Klah* observed dressed as an Indian: buckskin shirt, headband, braided hair, weapons, etc.
F451.2.8.1. To answer calls of *Pah-ho-ho Klah* hunter would go crazy — be lost for five days and five nights, the weather would be foggy and rainy for five days and five nights
F451.3.2.2.1. At dawning *Pah-ho-ho Klah* call out five times — depart; cf. F451.3.2.1. Dwarfs turn to stone at sunrise; cf. C311.8.1. Gods flee at approach of dawn; cf. C752.2.1. Tabu: supernatural creatures being abroad after sunrise; cf. E452.2. Ghost invisible during day
F451.3.2.2.2 *Pah-ho-ho Klah*[*Te-chum mah*?] are seen clearly as in a dream
F451.5.2.10. A *Pah-ho-ho Klah* observed making, straightening arrows
F451.5.2.10.1. *Pah-ho-ho Klah* [*Te-chum mah*] whistle like birds in the night, to cause travelers to get lost, to fall over a cliff, to die
F405.12.1. Fire keeps demons and the feared ones at bay
F564.5. Great sleepiness — before and after "seeing" the *Pah-ho-ho Klah*; cf. N776.3. Adventure(s) from having slept beneath a tree.

P. Society

P486.2.2. Hunter returns safely to camp
P716. Particular Places: [north central?] Oregon

R. Captives and Fugitives

R311. Tree refuge

S. Unnatural Cruelty

S143.5. Hunter becomes lost while hunting [due to great fog, rain]

W. Traits of Character

W230.1. A hunter
W230.4.1. *Pah-ho-ho Klah* [*Te-chum mah*] (dwarfs?)

Z. Miscellaneous Groups of Motifs

Z71.3.3. Five [lost 5 days and 5 nights] [raining, foggy weather 5 days and 5 nights][[call out 5 times]

3. BATTLE BETWEEN EAGLE AND OWL

A. Mythological Motifs

A2435.4.4.1. Eagle, as great hunter

B. Animals

B172.12. Owl, as a medicine man; cf. B511.5. Bird heals man
B264.2.1. Single-combat between eagle and owl
B810.9.1. Eagle
B810.11.3. Owl

D. Magic

D1021. Magic bearing-up feather; cf. D1380.22. Magic feather protects

P. Society

P557.8. Single-combat between eagle and owl occurs midair, up out of sight

Q. Rewards and Punishments

Q411.16. Death to loser in combat

PART THREE. TALES OF THE UMATILLA INDIANS

4A. TESTING THE GREAT *TAH* POWER OF THE WARRIOR

D. Magic

D1052.2. Magic buffalo robe; cf. E64.11. Resuscitation by magic robe — [gives shade, completely covers grave]
D1710.1. Possession of *Tah* or magic power
D1710.2. Personal *Tahs* of warrior [birds, animals — large and small] gather about grave
D1781.1. Magic results from singing *Tah* song; cf. D1275. Magic song

E. The Dead

E1.1.1. Warrior slain and cut to pieces comes back to life, whole
E1.3. Warrior comes back to life — resuscitates from burned remnant of bone
E31.1. Limbs, esp. head of dead are [by thought] reassembled — he revives
E55.6. Resuscitation directed by warrior's multiple *Tah* — personal magic [derived from animals and birds met on Spirit Quest]
E55.6.1. Resuscitation directed by Warrior's chief *Tah* — Buffalo
E232.5. Return from death to avenge treachery

F. Marvels

F677.2. Warrior locates villages, disguises self [and others] — enters freely, locates wife [twice]

H. Tests

H971.1.1. Burial of bone remnant of warrior under buffalo robe laid out by old woman; cf. N825. Old person as helper
H1151.2.3. Warrior task: stealing horses from enemy tribes [and more]
H1233.2. Old woman [relation] as helper of warrior on quest
H1501.2. Single combat fought to prove valor

J. The Wise and the Foolish

J1056. Old woman sent to village — to warn her people to place teepees to one side — not be killed

K. Deceptions

K1813.2. Disguised husband spies on his faithless wife
K2213.3.1. Faithless wife holds husband's leg — assists enemy warrior to kill husband
K2213.3.2. Faithless wife plots with paramour against husband's life
K2213.16. Treacherous wife coaxes husband to embrace — then clasps him tight, shouts for his capture

M. Ordaining the Future

M161.1.1. Vow to attack and kill wife and warrior from East
M161.2.1. Vow to seek revenge on treacherous wife

P. Society

P11.4.3. Chief chosen on basis of strength and exploits
P254. Treacherous wife's kin seek her death
P255. Kinsmen seize and tie up wife
P555.2.1. Warriors of warrior of East defeated — arms or legs torn off
P556.3. Warriors challenge each other to battle
P683. War, stealing as custom for Indians; cf. P557.4. Customs concerning single combat
P716. Particular Place: near Walla Walla, or the Umatilla country

Q. Rewards and Punishments

Q261.2. Treacherous wife punished

R. Captives and Fugitives

R133.1.1. Warrior successfully locates village where his wife lives [twice]
R227.4. Wife abandons less attractive husband for better man
R355.1. Kinsmen of treacherous wife visit scene of her treachery [husband's death]

S. Unnatural Cruelty

S112.1.1. Warrior burned to death — pyre of teepee poles; cf. K955. Murder by burning
S112.1.2. Treacherous wife and warior from East burned alive on great pyre; cf. Q414. Punishment: burning alive
S139.7.1. Death to warrior by slicing him to small pieces
S140.1. Abandonment of old woman

T. Sex

T231.6.	Treacherous widow marries slayer of husband
T236.1.	Woman enamored of unknown warrior in combat against her husband
T252.8.	Wife of warrior insists on going with him on foray

W. Traits of Character

W121.9.	Defeated warrior begs to be allowed to live
W212.	Eagerness [of warriors] for combat
W230.1.0.1.	Warrior, from the West
W230.1.0.2.	Opposing warrior, from the East
W230.1.1.	Many followers [of victor warrior]
W230.2.1.1.	A wife
W230.2.1.2.	Very old woman

Z. Miscellaneous Groups of Motifs

Z71.2.1.3.	Warrior and wife — travel *eastward*; warrior plus wife's kinfolk travel *eastward* — to scene of defeat; warrior plus wife's kinfolk travel *eastward* — to her village.
Z71.2.1.4.	Warrior returns *westward* to his village — tells of his betrayal and defeat; wife's relatives travel *westward* — back to village; warrior travels *westward* — to village; warrior returns *westward* — to his village
Z200.	Warrior becomes Chief, greatest of his tribe; cf. L122. Unsophisticated hero

4B. *TAHMAHNAWIS* POWER

B. Animals

B810.9.1.	An eagle

D. Magic

D1273.2.1.	*Tahmahnawis*, secret magic power
D1719.1.	Contest in magic
D1749.3.	Old shaman's magic diminishes with age
D1749.3.1.	Young shaman's magic is strongest (used less so far)
D1766.11.	Stronger *Tah* of younger shaman slays soaring eagle

H. Tests

H919.7.	Task imposed as a challenge
H939.5.	Task assigned by rival shaman
H953.	Old shaman fails at task
H991.1.	Young shaman defeats old shaman by means of stronger *Tah* power
H1049.4.	Task: shooting soaring eagle by means of shaman's *Tah*; cf. D2061.1. Kinds of death produced by magic

W. Traits of Character

W230.1.	An aged *Tahmahnawis* man; a young *Tahmahnawis* man.
W230.4.	A band of Umatilla hunters

5. A LEGEND OF DEEP LAKE, THE GRAND COULEE

B. Animals

B16.5.1.2.1.	Devastating (man-eating) lake-monster; cf. G308.2. Water-monster; cf. G308.4. Lake made dangerous by haunting serpent

C. Tabu

C614.1.	Forbidden direction of travel [hunting?]

F. Marvels

F713.7.	Remarkable lake teeming with fish
F759.9.	Great cliff

H. Tests

H1385.4.	Quest for vanished husband

P. Society

P486.4.	Fishing
P486.5.	Hunting
P486.6.	Digging roots
P716.	Particular Place: Grand Coulee

Q. Rewards and Punishments

Q552.3.5.1.	Punishment for greed: fisherman scorns small trout — seeks a big salmon — is drowned by that fish

S. Unnatural Cruelty

S131.2.	Large fish pulls fisherman into water — drowns him

T. Sex

T100.	Marriage

W. Traits of Character

W230.1.	A young man [from Snake River region]
W230.2.1.	A girl [an Okanogan]

6. THE DWARF MOUNTAIN PEOPLE

F. Marvels

F451.5.2.10.1.	Dwarfs call out in the woods, hoping to lead people astray; cf. F756.5. Extraordinary glen: mysterious shouting heard
F535.	Pygmy [NB: In *Motif Index* this term refers to a "dwarf," a remarkably small man — to distinguish from *dwarfs or other beings* who live in the woods and inhabit underground places]
F535.2.9.	Dwarf is no larger than a papoose
F535.3.3.	Dwarf dressed in a spotted fawn-skin
F535.4.4.	Dwarf is very old, face wrinkled
F535.7.1.	Dwarf armed with bow and arrows in a fawn-skin case
F535.8.	Abode of dwarf in caves in the rocks
F551.6.	Remarkable baby-size footprints of deer-tracker

F1088.5. Dwarf miraculously escapes from grasp of hunter — disappears; cf. D2095. Magic disappearance; also D2188.2. Person vanishes

P. Society

P251.4.2. Brothers agree to take dwarf to village to observe
P716. Particular place: hunting in the Blue Mountains

W. Traits of Character

W10.3. Hunter gives dwarf ride on horse; cf. W11.16. Generous hunter offers dwarf ride on horse
W230.1. A dwarf [little man]
W230.1.1. Three brothers

Z. Miscellaneous Groups of Motifs

Z71.1. Three [3 brothers]

PART FOUR. TALES OF THE WATLALA OR CASCADES INDIANS

7. BATTLE OF THE *AT-TE-YI-YI* AND *TO-QEE-NUT*

A. Mythological Motifs

A101.2. Spirit which rules
A522.1.3. Coyote as culture hero
A536.2. Coyote (culture-hero) fights as ally of the Wolf brothers; cf. N810. Supernatural helpers
A536.2.1. Coyote aids Salmon-youth in struggle against the Wind brothers
A546.1. Coyote regrets killing of Salmon-Chief, who was "a good man"
A950. Dual tracks where wolves stood is set into rocks on Washington side of Columbia River, at Wishram, near the Tumwater
A1135.1.2. Origin of cold: Sister of winds escapes into river
A1136. Origin of warm weather: hero [Salmon-youth] defeats Wind brothers; Chinook winds to blow instead of cold
A1599.17. Origin of the victory call in games or battles
A2433.3.13.1. Why wolves live in Cascade Mountains
A2484.2. Why salmon come plentifully as they do

B. Animals

B264.6 Representative single combat between animals [between Salmon and the Winds]
B810.3.2. Wolf(s) [5 Wolf brothers]
B810.3.3. Coyote(s)
B810.13. Birds
B810.18.1. Salmon [Chief] (and all fish or Salmon people)
B810.18.2. Salmon-youth
B810.24.2. Animal people(s) [Wolf, Coyote, Fox people kill Salmon people]

D. Magic

D124.2.4. Magic oil
D1017.2. Magic salmon oil

D1242.1. Magic water
D1335.18. Magical oil poured underfoot gives strength
D1810.14. Magic knowledge of identity of Salmon-youth; cf. F643. Marvelous presentiment of coming of Salmon-youth
D1832.1. Magic strength and growth come by cold water baths in winter
D1832.1.1. Magic strength by bathing, by sweating, cold water
D1835.7. Magic strength from "practicing his strength while going"
D2144.2. Contest of heat and cold. Hero [Salmon] and the Wolves [Winds] wrestle. If the Winds win, ice and cold will be everywhere always

F. Marvels

F436.1. The North [Northeast] Winds [5 brothers and a sister]
F436.2. Chinook wind [Salmon-wind], a warm wind
F610.2.1. Remarkably strong youth [salmon-youth]
F611.1.14.1. Salmon-youth, son of Salmon-chief, as strong hero
F611.3.1. Strong hero practices uprooting trees; cf. F621. Strong man: tree-puller
F611.3.1.1. Strong hero practices uprooting trees, lifting, pulling, running, jumping, throwing rocks
F617. Mighty wrestler(s)
F642.2.0.1. Strong youth throws enormous stone great distance [to middle of the Columbia River]
F645.3. Marvelously wise grandmother [relates to young salmon of mishaps suffered by parents][marvelous presentiment of coming of Salmon-youth]
F645.4. Marvelously wise grandmother tells magical actions necessary to obtain revenge
F715.10. Frozen *n-Che-wana* as site of wrestling
F757.2.1. Five Wind brothers live in cave [at *Wah-pe-us*, near Celilo]; cf. A1122. Cave of winds; R315. Cave as refuge
F930.9. Heavy rains cause Salmon egg to hatch, to slip into the water
F962.13.1. Extraordinary darkness and heavy rains; cf. D2140. Magic control of elements

H. Tests

H1381.2.2.3. Grandmother sought [found] by young Salmon
H1562.9. Test of strength: wrestling

J. The Wise and the Foolish

J321.5. Wolves fail to lick up last salmon egg, so abandon it
J641.2. Salmon advises his wife and children to flee in event of his defeat

K. Deceptions

K619.2.1. Oil put on ice [or applied to feet] prevents slipping

L. Reversal of Fortune

L101. Umpromising hero; cf. L111.2. Foundling hero
L101.2. Unpromising hero: third brother bests Salmon-chief
L431.4. Sneering brothers disregard power of young challenger
L311. Weak (small) hero overcomes large fighter
L333. Sister escapes by diving through hole in ice into river

M. Ordaining the Future

M325.1. Prophecy of coming of the human race

P. Society

P555.4. Two Wind brothers are defeated in wrestling by *To-qee-nut*
P555.5. *To-qee-nut* defeated and killed by third Wind brother
P555.5.2. Five Wind brothers are killed in wrestling with Salmon-youth hero
P556.3. Challenge made to wrestle on frozen river ice [Wolves challenge Salmon-chief to battle] [Wolves challenge Salmon-youth to battle]
P557.4.4.2. Youngest Wind brother afraid, must fight slayer of his four older brothers

Q. Rewards and Punishments

Q469.14. Punishment: lame sister struck hard on naked buttocks with thorny rosebush
Q471.3. Punishment: defecating in old slave woman's hair; cf. R51. Mistreatment of prisoners; cf. P672.3. Rubbing shaved head of hero with cow dung as insult

R. Captives and Fugitives

R51.1.1. Slave woman denied food, clothes, warmth
R327.1. One salmon egg rolls into deep crack in rocks — escapes destruction

S. Unnatural Cruelty

S110.6. Children of Salmon-Chief murdered by the Wolves
S116.7. Eggs of Salmon-woman are destroyed by being crushed; cf. C544. Tabu: crushing eggs; cf. J622. Preventing the birth of enemies
S139.1.1. Murder of Salmon-chief's wife by "bursting her open;" cf. P555.2. Corpses of dead foes dismembered
S302.2. At defeat of hero, all his children are killed/beheaded

T. Sex

T500. Wife of slain hero with child [filled with eggs]

W. Traits of Character

W212.3. Salmon-youth shows strength, heart, eagerness for combat
W230.2.1.1. A slave [woman]; [sister to grandmother]
W230.2.2.2. Sister(s) [crippled sister]
W230.2.3. Grandmother

Z. Miscellaneous Groups of Motifs

Z71.0.1. Two [2 Wind brothers defeated]
Z71.2.0. Four [4 whirls of foes]
Z71.3.5. Five [5 Wolf brothers] [5 days] [5 days, 5 baskets of oil] [5 Wind brothers] [5 whirls {wrestling "falls"} of foes]
Z71.4. Six [6 months or "moons"]

Z71.5. Seven [7 times foe whirled]
Z71.16.15. Fifty [stronger than 50 men]

8. ORIGIN OF THE HORSE

A. Mythological Motifs

A1881.0.2. Horse was originally found in lakes

B. Animals

B211.1.3.1.1. Horses understand our language [their forebear was a human]
B312.5.1. At roundup woman-mare was captured (later released)
B606. Marriage to horse; cf. B611.3. Horse paramour
B632. Two colts result from horse-human marriage
B810.7.2. Horse

D. Magic

D131.1.1. Partial transformation: woman to horse
D131.1.2. Woman is transformed into a mare — bears many colts

P. Society

P486.4. Horse roundups

W. Traits of Character

W230.1.1. A chief — whose wife has disappeared
W230.1.2. A hunter — espies woman-horse
W230.1.3. An Indian man-stallion
W230.2.1. An Indian woman
W231.1.1. A council — spies out human-horse marrieds

Z. Miscellaneous Groups of Motifs

Z71.2.1.5. Direction: the East, somewhere
Z73.2.4. Season: autumn

9. HOW A WATER-BALL WAS MADE

D. Magic

Dl171.11.1. Magic basket [open-weave, holds water]
D1171.11.2. Magic water-basket
D1209.9. Magic dip-net [holds water for magician for sweat house]
D1209.10. Magic ball [made of water, carried on shoulder]
D1209.10.1. When finger is thrust into water-ball, then water runs out
D1719.1.5. Contest in magic to fetch water sans bucket
D1719.10. Person(s) with magic powers carry water in open-weave basket(s)
D1731.1. Spirit quest; cf. C423.1. Tabu: disclosing source of magic power; cf. also C423.4. Tabu: uttering secrets heard from spirits; cf. also C423.6; C426
D1739.3. Magic power from seal — given in a dream to magician is the mystery of the seal's *airsac* and the power to make a water-ball

W. Traits of Character

W231.1.1. Three men-sweatbathers

Z. Miscellaneous Groups of Motifs

Z71.1. Three [3 men] [3 magic feats]

10A. A CASCADE LEGEND

D. Magic

D551. Transformation [back to life] buy eating; cf. D1793. Magic results from eating and drinking

D905. Magic storm: thunder, lightning, rain — on fifth day; cf. D2141.1. Storm produced by magic

E. The Dead

E1. Brother comes to life

H. Tests

H1556.2.1. Test of fidelity through submitting brother to temptations by sister-in-law

L. Reversal of Fortune

L101. Unpromising hero (male Cinderella) — younger brother

M. Ordaining the Future

M185.1. Vow by younger brother to live and not be bad any more: not steal goods, not steal women, etc.

M201.2.1. Covenant confirmed by giving gifts

M301.22. Younger brother as prophet

M364.4.2. Brother's resurrection will occur five days after death

Q. Rewards and Punishments

Q411.0.1.1. Adulterer killed; cf. Q233.1. Death as punishment for yielding to temptations of sister-in-law

Q551.8.3.1. Putridity of corpse within five days

S. Unnatural Cruelty

S115.4. Adulterer brother shot with five poisoned arrows

T. Sex

T332.2. Husband sends wife to tempt his brother

W. Traits of Character

W2.1. Goodness, etc. in character [younger brother]

W230.2.1. Chief's wife [as temptress, as witness]

W230.2.2. Multiple wives

W231.1.1. A Cascade Indian chief and his younger brother

Z. Miscellaneous Groups of Motifs

Z71.3. Five [5 days dead] [5 poisoned arrows] [putrescence within 5 days] [storm on 5th day]

10B. A LEGEND OF THE CASCADE TRIBE

D. Magic

D551. Transformation [back to life] by eating; cf. D1793. Magic results from eating and drinking

D905. Magic storm: thunder, great wind — on fifth day; cf. D2141.1. Storm produced by magic

E. The Dead

E.1. Younger brother comes to life

H. Tests

H1556.2.1. Test of fidelity through submitting younger brother to temptations by Chief's wife [sister-in-law]

J. The Wise and the Foolish

J1782.9. Voice of dead younger brother causes fear to elder brother

L. Reversal of Fortune

L101. Unpromising hero (male Cinderella) — younger brother

M. Ordaining the Future

M185.2. Vow by younger brother — to be good henceforth

M201.2. Covenant confirmed by big feast

M301.22. Younger brother as prophet

M364.4.2. Younger brother's resurrection will occur five days after death

Q. Rewards and Punishments

Q411.0.1.1. Adulterer killed; cf. Q233.1. Death as punishment for yielding to temptations of sister-in-law

Q551.8.3.1. Putrescence of corpse within five days

S. Unnatural Cruelty

S115.4. Adulterer [younger] brother shot with five poisoned arrows

T. Sex

T332.2. Husband sends wife to tempt his younger brother

W. Traits of Character

W2.1. Goodness in character [younger brother]

W230.2.1. Chief's wife — [as temptress, as witness]

W230.2.2. Multiple wives [4-5]

W230.1.1. A Cascade Indian chief and his younger brother

Z. Miscellaneous Groups of Motifs

Z71.3. Five [4-5 wives] [5 days dead] [5 poisoned arrows] [putresence within 5 days] [storm on 5th day]

11A. THE STRONG BOY OF THE CASCADES

A. Mythological Motifs

A977.5.5. Strong Boy places large rock [Castle Rock?] and sits upon it, while training for strength

C. Tabu

C752.1.3.1. Tabu: single person [male] to enter Chief's house after sunset

F. Marvels

F517.1. Youth's feet are bigger than his father's
F531.3.7. Giant has feet "half the length of a lodgepole;" also G365. Ogre monstrous as to feet
F611.3.1.1. Strong hero practices to become strong

H. Tests

H36.1. Recognition [of son] by footprints as large or larger than Chief's
H903. Youth trains to be strong
H931.1.2. Three strong men sent to bring back the Chief's son
H1556.6.1. Test of fidelity of wives: sand is spread nightly about house to show footprints of any intruder; cf. T381.0.2. Wife(s) imprisoned in tower (house) to preserve chastity; also cf. T383. Other futile attempts to keep wife(s) chaste.

J. The Wise and the Foolish

J1146. Detection by strewing sand. Trespasser [son of Chief] leaves huge footprints in the sand

K. Deceptions

K514.2. Boy-baby passed off as a girl to prevent its murder

L. Reversal of Fortune

L142.3. Son surpasses father in [war] skill and strength: single-handedly defeats the attacking army

P. Society

P10.2. *Tos-cas wo-hah*, a Chief — of village near Bridge of the Gods
P236.4. Strong youth deposes evil father, breaks evil power of old chief
P461.5. Chief and warriors set out in a hundred canoes
P716. Particular Places: near Bridge of the Gods; near White Salmon

R. Captives and Fugitives

R227.2.1. Flight from feared husband
R228.1. Infant boy taken to White Salmon to save his life

S. Unnatural Cruelty

S11. Cruel father
S11.3.3.3. Chief kills all sons as soon as they are born
S11.4.7. Father wages war against unknown son
S174.1. Chief's messengers defeated — sent away with *crushed* arms

S174.2. Son defeats father — crushes his father's bones with his hands
S322.1.5.3. Chief, fearful of a son as a rival, puts all infant sons to death

T. Sex

T145. Polygamous marriages
T145.1.4. Two hundred wives
T224.2. Chief wishes to satisfy "baby's longing, allows wife and infant [son] to return to White Salmon for visit
T586.2.1.1. Chief has many daughters, but not one son
T689. Mother is frightened that her son will be discovered and killed by cruel father

W. Traits of Character

W138. Falsehood: wife lies to husband to preserve life of infant son
W230.1. A Chief
W230.1.1. A boy infant
W230.1.1.1 Three strong men
W230.2.1. *Ni-ti-it*, a White Salmon wife

Z. Miscellaneous Groups of Motifs

Z71.1. Three [3 strong men]
Z71.3. Five [5 canoes loaded with gifts]
Z71.15.6. One-hundred [100 canoes]
Z71.15.7. Two hundred [200 wives]

11B. A CASCADE INDIAN LEGEND

A. Mythological Motifs

A969.10. Origin of Castle Rock: carried by youthful hero to present location

D. Magic

D1067.2. Magic cap
D1381.26.1. Magic cap protects from attack
D2061.2.1. Death-giving glance [at cap]; cf. G264.1. Woman is death of all who behold her
D2125.1. Big-footed Chief able to walk on water

F. Marvels

F517.1. Person unusual as to his feet; cf. G365. Ogre monstrous as to feet; also cf. F531.3.7. Giant has feet "three feet long"
F611.3.1.1. Strong hero practices to become strong
F771.0.1. Large *round* lodge

H. Tests

H36.1. Recognition [of son] by footprints as large or larger than Chief's
H919.7. Tasks assigned at instigation of Chief
H931.1.2. Strong sent to capture son [fatal capture]
H1556.6.1.1. Test of fidelity of wives: sand or dirt is spread about house to show footprints of any intruder

J. The Wise and the Foolish

J1146.	Detection by strewn sand. Trespasser [son of Chief] leaves huge footprints in the sand

K. Deceptions

K601.3.	To prevent father killing infant son, mother lies that it's a girl

L. Reversal of Fortune

L311.6.	Single youth overcomes two strong attackers, breaks their arms

R. Captives and Fugitives

R227.2.1.	Flight from feared husband

S. Unnatural Cruelty

S11.	Cruel father
S11.3.3.3.	Cruel father kills all sons as soon as they are born
S11.4.7.	Father wages war against unknown son
S110.2.1.	Woman kills all men who seek to slay son
S322.1.5.3.	Chief, fearful of a son as rival, puts all infant sons to death

T. Sex

T52.10.	A Hood River [*Nom-i-neet*] wife
T145.	Polygamous marriages
T224.1.	Wife allowed to return to her home with infant for a visit
T586.2.1.1.	Chief has many daughters, but not one son

W. Traits of Character

W138.	Falsehood: wife lies to husband to preserve life of infant son
W230.1.	A Cascade Indian Chief
W230.4.	Many wives
W231.1.1.	A boy infant
W231.1.1.	Two strong men

Z. Miscellaneous Groups of Motifs

Z71.0.1.	Two [2 strong men]
Z16.14.20.	Twenty-five [son is 25 years old]
Z71.16.2.	Ten [10 years old]
Z71.16.17.	*Many* men, *many* canoes

COMPARATIVE NOTES TO OTHER PLATEAU INDIAN TALES

These comparative notes cite narratives similar to those found herein from nearby tribes over the Plateau Region. The tribes and the titles of printed collections of traditional narratives used hereafter follow.

Yakima

Beavert, Virginia 1974. *The way it was* (*Anaku Iwacha*) (*Yakima legends*), The Consortium of Johnson O'Malley Committees of Region IV, State of Washington. Yakima, Washington.

Klickitat

Jacobs, Melville 1929. *Northwest Sahaptin texts, 1*, University of Washington Publications in Anthropology, 2, No. 5. Seattle: University of Washington Press.

Jacobs, Melville 1969. *Northwest Sahaptin texts*, Columbia University Contributions to Anthropology, 19, Part I. New York: AMS Press.

Tenino (also Umatilla, Cascade [*Watlala*] narratives)

Hines, Donald M. 1991. *The forgotten tribes*. . . . Issaquah, Washington.

Nez Perce

Hines, Donald M. 1984. *Tales of the Nez Perce*. Fairfield, WA.: Ye Galleon Press.

Mayer, Theresa 1917. Folk-tales of Sahaptin tribes. *Folk-tales of Salishan and Sahaptin tribes*, Memoirs of the American Folk-Lore Society, 11. New York: American Folk-lore Society.

Slickpoo Sr., Allen P. *Nu Mee Poom Tit Wah Tit* (*Nez Perce legends*). NP: Nez Perce Tribe of Idaho.

Spinden, Herbert J. 1917. Nez Perce Tales. *Folk-tales of Salishan and Sahaptin tribes*, Memoirs of the American Folk-Lore Society, 11 (New York: American Folk-Lore Society.

Coeur d'Alene

Reichard, Gladys A. 1947. *An analysis of Coeur D'Alene Indian myths*. Memoirs of the American Folklore Society, 41. Philadelphia: American Folklore Society.

Teit, James A. 1917. Coeur d'Alene Tales. *Folk-tales of Salishan and Sahaptin tribes*, Memoirs of the American Folk-Lore Society, 11. New York: American Folk-Lore Society.

Kutenai

Boas, Franz 1918. *Kutenai tales*, BAE 59. Washington, D.C.: U.S. Government Printing Office.

Lillooet

Hill-Tout, Charles 1978. *The Squamish and the Lillooet, II, The Salish people*. Vancouver, Talonbooks.

Okanagon

Gould, Marian K. 1917. Okanagon Tales. *Folk-tales of Salishan and Sahaptin tribes*, Memoirs of the American Folk-Lore Society, 11. New York: American Folk-Lore Society.

Hill-Tout, Charles 1978. *The Thompson and the Okanagan*, I, *The Salish people*. Vancouver: Talonbooks.

Hines, Donald M. 1976. *Tales of the Okanogans*. Fairfield, Washington, Ye Galleon Press.

Teit, James A. 1917. Okanogan Tales. *Folk-tales of Salishan and Sahaptin tribes*, Memoirs of the American Folk-Lore Society, 11. New York: American Folk-Lore Society.

Thompson

Hill-Tout, Charles 1978. *The Thompson and the Okanagan*, I, *The Salish People*. Vancouver: Talonbooks.

Teit, James A. 1917. Thompson Tales. *Folk-tales of Salishan and Sahaptin tribes*, Memoirs of the American Folk-Lore Society, 11. New York: American Folk-Lore Society.

Teit, James A. 1898. *Traditions of the Thompson River Indians of British Columbia*, Memoirs of the American Folk-Lore Society, 6. New York: American Folk-Lore Society.

Pend D'Oreille

Teit, James A. 1917. Pend d'Oreille Tales," *Folk-tales of Salishan and Sahaptin tribes*, Memoirs of the American Folklore Society, 11. New York: American Folk-Lore Society.

PART ONE. TALES OF THE TENINO-WARM SPRINGS INDIANS

1. *NASH-LAH*

YAKIMA Beavert 1974: 28-31; KLICKITAT Jacobs 1969: esp. 65-66; NEZ PERCE Farrand 1917: 149-151 (2 versions); Hines 1984: 43-45; Slickpoo 1972: 206; Spinden 1917: 200-201; COEUR D'ALENE Reichard 1947: 68-71; Teit 1917: 121-122 (2 versions); OKANOGAN Hines 1976: 116-117; PEND D'ORIELLE Teit 1917: 115-117 (2 versions).

2. THE *PAH-HO-HO KLAH*

TENINO Hines 1991: #2 "The *Pah-ho-ho Klah*;" also #10 "The Dwarf Mountain People."

3. BATTLE BETWEEN EAGLE AND OWL

Frequently told, this tale of rivalry over possession of a wife, of displays of extraordinary power, usually depicts eagle vying against owl, but perhaps more often skunk. Both are powerful figures and possess much magic.

YAKIMA Beavert 1974: 76; KLICKITAT Jacobs 1969: 42-43; Jacobs 1929: 207-215; NEZ PERCE Hines 1984: 151-158; Slickpoo 1972 29-36; COEUR D'ALENE Reichard 1947: 158-171; KUTENAI Boas 1918: 40, also pp. 230-243 (2 versions); OKANOGAN Hines 1976: 75-79; THOMPSON Teit 1898: 59-61.

PART TWO. TALES OF THE UMATILLA INDIANS

4A. TESTING THE GREAT *TAH* POWER OF THE WARRIOR

(none)

4B. *TAHMAHNAWIS* POWER

(none)

5. A LEGEND OF DEEP LAKE, THE GRAND COULEE

(none)

6. THE DWARF MOUNTAIN PEOPLE

Traditional accounts of hunters lost or otherwise sidetracked by supernatural elements were widely related as by the Yakimas and the Klickitats. These accounts relate of calls like birds in the night, supposedly made by "little people of the mountains," essentially unseen or invisible; of voices in the darkness, of calls in the darkness which threatened to lead Indians "crazy," even to lead them over a cliff to their deaths.

TENINO Hines 1991: #2 "The *Pah-ho-ho Klah*;" and #10 "The Dwarf Mountain People."

PART THREE. TALES OF THE *WATLALA* ORCASCADES INDIANS

7. BATTLE OF THE *AT-TE-YI-YI* AND *TO-QEE-NUT*

This narrative details the magical struggle between forces wishing long and extremely cold winters, and others who wished for short and mild winters in the vicinity of Celilo Falls, the locale of the Wascos and other tribes.

YAKIMA Beavert 1974: 10-24; KLICKITAT Jacobs 1969: 30-32 (two texts); NEZ PERCE Farrand 1917: 144-148, esp. 147-148; Hines 1984: 120-127, esp. pp. 124-127; Slickpoo 1972: 2-6; 10-16 (two texts); COEUR D'ALENE Reichard 1947: 189-190; Teit 1917: 124 (two texts); KUTENAI Boas 1918: 178-183; LILLOOET Hill-Tout 1978: 154-155; OKANOGAN Gould 1917: 104-105; Hines 1976: 42-47; Teit 1917: 74; THOMPSON Teit 1898: 55-56; Teit 1917: 21.

8. ORIGIN OF THE HORSE

TENINO Hines #4 "Origin of the Horse;" THOMPSON Teit 1898: 92-93; Teit 1917: 53 [Teit cites comparable versions from regions east of the Rocky Mountains.]

9. HOW A WATER-BALL WAS MADE

(none)

10A A CASCADE LEGEND

TENINO Hines 1991 #10A "A Cascade Legend;" also #10B "A Legend of the Cascade Tribe;" LILLOOET Hill-Tout 1978: 146-147; THOMPSON Teit 1898: 68-69; Teit 1917: 45-46.

10B. A LEGEND OF THE CASCADE TRIBE

TENINO Hines 1991: #10A "A Cascade Legend;" also #10B "A Legend of the Cascade Tribe;" LILLOOET Hill-Tout 1978: 146-147; THOMPSON Teit 1898: 68-69; Teit 1917: 45-46.

11A. THE STRONG BOY OF THE CASCADES

COWLITZ Jacobs 1969: 123-124; TENINO Hines #11A "The Strong Boy of the Cascades;" also #11B "A Cascade Indian Legend;" KUTENAI Boas 1918: 28-33.

11B. A CASCADE INDIAN LEGEND

COWLITZ Jacobs 1969: 123-124; TENINO Hines #11A "The Strong Boy of the Cascades;" also #11B "A Cascade Indian Legend;" KUTENAI Boas 1918: 28-33.

LIST OF INFORMANTS

Listed below are the several names, if known, of each informant and the narratives ascribed to them. A brief biographical sketch is included for each informant, if data was available.

1. NARRATOR AND/OR DATE UNKNOWN: 3, 4A, 4B, 5, 6, 7.

2. *Ah-nah-chu Pick-wah-pah*, "Behind the Rock," an intelligent young man of the Warm Springs tribe, gave McWhorter his experience with the *Pah-ho-ho Klah*: "calling," "signaling" or "answering." No date cited: 2.

3. *Che-pos To-cos*, (Owl Child), also known as *Shat-Taw-Wee* (Leader in Battle), whose English Name was Alec McCoy. In his autobiography, Owl Child recalls: "I was born at the Dalles, Oregon; we call the place Wasco. I was born on the site of the old Wishom village which was burned by the soldiers during the Yakima War, 1855-56. My father, *Pul-Kus*, was of the Wishom tribe, while my mother, *An-nee-swolla* was a Wasco woman. Owl Child was, in his own right, an accomplished raconteur. And he dwelt at a place and a time when Watlala Indians were likely met, their oral lore heard. While studies are extant on the retentative tenacity of oral tradition, few or no studies are extant on the ability of a tale-teller from outside a tribal group to faithfully, in detail, relate that tribe's oral lore: 9, 10A, 10B, 11A, 11B.

4. *Lu-pah'-kin* (also known as Caesar Williams). According to McWhorter, "*Lu-pah'-kin* was an hereditary chief of the Warm Springs tribe; he was the son of Capt. "Dry Creek Billie," a noted warrior and scout for the government. *Lu-pah'-kin* married a prominent Yakima woman and cast his lot with that tribe, where he became a recognized leader at every tribal gathering where old-time customs were in evidence. I first became acquainted with him in October 1903, every since which time we were close friends until his death in the late autumn of 1924. . . . He was a man of strong Dreamer religious convictions, with strong, premonition tendencies:" 1.

5. Chief Meninock (originally *Menine-okt*). McWhorter states: "Chief Meninock belonged to the *Skein-tla-ma* tribe, residing on the *n-Che-wana* opposite the mouth of the Deschutes River." According to Spier, *Wishram Ethnography*, the peoples residing opposite the mouth of the Deschutes River were the *Sk!in* Indians:" 8.

NOTES TO THE NARATIVES

PART ONE
INTRODUCTION: THE SETTING, PROVENANCE AND ORGANIZATION OF THE TALES OF THE TENINOS AND NEARBY MID-COLUMBIA RIVER INDIAN NATIONS

1. See "Wishram" in Hodge, F.W., ed. 1959. *Handbook of American Indians North of Mexico*. New York: Pageant Books, Inc., II, p. 965.
2. For these notes we have employed Spier, L. and E. Sapir 1930. *Wishram ethnography*, UWPA, No. 3:151-300. Seattle.
3. See "*Watlala*" in Swanton, J.R., ed. 1952. *The Indian tribes of North America*, BBAE 145: 476. Washington, D.C.
4. See the biographical note on Chief Meninock, in List of Informants above.

PART TWO
THE TENINO-WARM SPRINGS INDIANS

I. THE TRADITIONAL NARRATIVES

5. The "five sisters" which Coyote carries in his stomach (bowel), who are wise and tell him things, are his dung.
6. *Nash-lah* was the wife of *Cli-colah*, and the couple lived in the Tumwater [upper or head of the former Columbia River rapids] at what is now Fall Bridge [Wishram, WA] Columbia River. The last time they were seen was on the rocks at the river's edge, on the north side of the stream. *Nash-lah* was combing her husband's hair, which was long and flowing. *Cli-colah* was captured by *Nash-lah*, who loved him and took him as her husband. One version of the legend is that the couple were seen with a papoose, a child born to them.

   Another version says they live in the Tumwater. The last time they were seen was on an island nearby. The man had long flowing hair, as also did the woman. The woman was fine looking. Two little beings dwell in the lake at the source of the Naches River.

   It is at night when oftimes *Kola-koola* (*Cli-colah*) leaves a gift, an arrowpoint or other stone implement, such as a medicine mortar, under the pillow or headrest of the sleeper in camp. *Lu-pah-hin* (narrator of the tale) was the recipient of such a last-named gift in 1919, the third night in camp at a tribal gathering on Rock Creek, Washington. The mortar, of fine, blue-colored stone, was "clean and nice" when found at breaking of the camp. Rigid inquiry failed to find an owner, and it was declared to have been placed there for the sleeper by *Kola-koola*. Such a gift must be carefully cared for, otherwise it will mysteriously disappear, taken back by *Kola-koola*. It should never be sold, traded or disposed of in any way.

7. If described elsewhere as a female water sprite, the tale quickly focuses on *Nash-lah* as a male water ogre (DH).

8. The *Pah-ho-ho Klah* are allied if not identical with the *Te-chum mah*: "ground people," or "belonging to the ground."

9. The Klamath Indians have legends of a fairy-dwarf called *Ch-caka* who can live alike in the water or on the land. They are a "powerful people; can go fast like the lightning."

10. Accounts by hunters, lost or otherwise sidetracked in their travels, relate of calls like birds in the night, made by the "little people of the mountains" essentially unseen or invisible. Also heard are mysterious voices in the darkness, of calls in the darkness to lead Indians "crazy," even lead them over a cliff to their deaths. That this narrative is set in the real world, a factual milieu helps mark this as a legendary narrative. See also in this volume #10 "The Dwarf Mountain People."

11. A fragment of a Warm Springs Indian tale. Told by *Lu-pah-hin*, date unknown.

II. "THE TENINO INDIANS"

12. Reprinted, by permission of the publisher, from Murdock, G. P. 1980. The Tenino Indians. *Ethnology* 19:129-149.

13. We have taken the liberty of bringing to Murdock's original essay comparative notes from Spier, L. and E. Sapir, *Wishram Ethnography*, previously cited. Citations are given as "Spier 1930: p.___." Other sources cited here are listed in the bibliography at the close of this volume.

14. Spier 1930:162 cites from Ross, *Adventures*, of "*Wai-yampam*" who were located at ". . . the head of the Long Narrows in 1811-1813." And on page 169 Lewis and Clark are cited as mentioning the *Wahhowpum* (*Waiya'mpum*) located ". . . on the north shore near Rock Creek, twenty-four miles above the mouth of the Deschutes River."

15. Murdock expresses reservations about this point in Murdock, G. P. 1938. Notes on the Tenino, Molala, and Paiute of Oregon. *American Anthropology* n.s. 40: 395-402.

16. It is not clear whether Murdock ever visited the Indian fishery at the Celilo Falls of the Columbia River. Indeed, the Wasco tribe was probably located directly westward of the Teninos, while opposite the Wishrams peopled the Washington side of the Columbia River.

17. Spier 1930:167. The Klickitats were located on the Washington side of the Columbia River westward of the Wishrams, and were centered about present-day White Salmon and Underwood, Washington.

18. Spier 1930:168 f..
19. Spier 1930:174.
20. Spier 1930:182-184 lists the varieties of vegetal foods taken by Wishram women.
21. Spier 1930:202-203 cites the earth lodge as a winter house, and the mat lodge as a summer lodge and fish-drying shed.
22. Spier 1930:248-249 explains this early feast as a "First Salmon Rite," noted by Lewis and Clark at the Dalles, April 19, 1806.
23. Spier 1930:224 affirms this.
24. Spier 1930:224 notes that the Wishram were almost entirely stay-at-home middlemen.
25. But see note 8 above.
26. But Murdock failed to understand how the Dalles, especially the falls at Celilo, barred river crossings except far downstream from, or still upriver from the John Day or Deschutes River estuaries.
27. Spier 1930:189.
28. Spier 1930:188-189.
29. Spier 1930:199 notes that eagle feathers were used on war arrows, but feathers of the mountain hawk on hunting arrows.
30. Spier 1930:205.
31. Spier 1930:190.
32. Neither cedar nor "timber" oaks and maples are found in the sere, treeless environs of the Tenino and the Umatilla peoples.
33. Spier 1930:176-188 cites the use of "flax fiber."
34. Spier 1930:192. Neither the Wasco nor the Wishram made coiled baskets according to one source. But the Klickitat apparently did.
35. Spier 1930:182 notes that gathering of "all vegetal products" was a feminine task.
36. Spier 1930:221.
37. Spier 1930:221.
38. Spier 1930:218.
39. Spier 1930:217.
40. Spier 1930:217-218.
41. But Spier 1930:218 notes only of the *two* fathers.
42. Spier 1930:218 notes that the purchase price might be horses or property or money.
43. Spier 1930:219.
44. Spier 1930:218.
45. Spier 1930:218.

46. Spier 1930:220.

47. Spier 1930:229-240 describes a child's training for his "spirit experience" when 6-7 years old and under the direction of an "inspector." But see p. 257, the punishment for falling asleep.

48. Spier 1930:221-224.

49. Spier 1930:211 notes of the "strongly marked" class feeling among the Wishram.

50 Spier 1930:211 notes that [as in 1875] "several men were simultaneously chiefs."

51. Spier 1930:212-213.

52. Spier 1930:236 notes that "the spirits from which power was obtained were animals, birds, reptiles, insects, and fish, that is, inhabitants of the physical world, not the physical world itself."

53. See note 41 above.

54. Spier 1930:240 notes that "some" got 5-6 spirits.

55. Spier 1930:240.

56. Spier 1930:242 notes that shamans possessed "strong spirits" of the wolf, eagle, rattlesnake, etc.

57. But Spier 1930:236 notes that "secret societies did not exist among the Wishram, nor were there shamans' organizations."

58. Spier 1930:244.

59. Spier 1930:246 makes no mention of a diagnostic spirit, nor its role in a cure--and no tube was used.

60. Spier 1930:246.

61. Spier 1930:247-248.

62 Cf. Spier 1930:251-252.

63. But Murdock makes no mention of the Indian Shaker faith, a revelatory, highly ritualized worship with numerous followers on the Yakima Confederated Tribal Reservation.

PART THREE
THE UMATILLA INDIANS

I. INTRODUCTORY NOTES

(none)

II. TALES OF THE UMATILLA INDIANS

64. See "Umatilla," in Swanton, J.R., ed. 1952. *The Indian Tribes of North America*, BBAE 145: p. 474. Washington, D.C.
65. A Umatilla legend. Informant and date not given.
66. A Umatilla legend. Informant and date not given.
67. As given in this narrative, the dwarfs are the counterparts of the *Te-chum* of the Yakimas.
68. A Umatilla legend, informant and date not given.

PART FOUR
THE *WATLALA* OR CASCADES INDIANS

I. INTRODUCTORY NOTES

69. Useful sources on the Cascades or *Watlala* Indians include: Spier, L. and E. Sapir, 1930. *Wishram Ethnography*.

    "*Watlala*," in Swanton, J.R., ed. 1952. *The Indian Tribes of North America*, BBAE 145:476.

    "*Watlala*," in Hodge, F.W., ed. 1910. *Handbook of American Indians north of Mexico*, BBAE 30, Part 2:922.
70. To separate the confusing multiple-possible uses of Cascades, we indicate the lower part of the Columbia River rapids as "cascades;" we indicate the tribe as "Cascades Indians;" we indicate the range of mountains as "Cascades Mountains."
71. Lewis and Clark mention a village at the head of the "cascades" in 1805, behind which were ponds. See Hosmer, II, 53-54.
72. See Spier, *Wishram Texts*, p. 22.

II. TALES OF THE *WATLALA* INDIANS

73. *At-te-yi-yi*, "cold northeast wind," is the most deadly of all winds. It is sometimes called *Ta-ye-a*.
74. McWhorter consistently employs the spelling "Wishom" for the tribal name and, here, the modern town-site, "Wishram."

75. *Wah-pe-us* is literally "catching fish with a dip net." It is located at or near *Skein*, "cradle-board," in the *n-Che-wana*, not far from Celilo. Salmon were also gaffed at *Wah-pe-us*, those that "jump."

76. The oils of the dog-salmon, and of the eel possess the property of preventing slipping on the ice. Either of these oils applied to the sole of the moccasin insures the wearer a secure footing on the smoothest of ice. The dog-salmon is the *Qee-nut*, or royal chinook salmon, at a certain period. The *um-to-li*, or *m-to-la* is the *Qee-nut* at spawning.

77. *We-now-y-yi*, "Young Chinook-wind," is a powerful, warm wind from a distance. In the legend young Chinook-wind is personified as *Qee-nut*, the chinook salmon, and the son of *To-qee-nut*, the Chief of Salmon, Chief of all the fishes.

78. In some versions of this legend, even in the same tribe, as with the Klickitats, this slave woman held by the *At-te-yi-yi* was *We-now-y-yi-ats*, a sister to *We-now-y-yi*, the young Chinook wind.

79. In this narrative it is noticeable that *Ats-te-yi-yi*, the crippled sister, does not pour water for the purpose of forming ice that the enemy of her brothers might not stand as she does in "Battle of Cold-Wind and Chinook-Wind," told by the Wascos.

80. The peculiar cry or call is rendered by placing the hand over the mouth and by rapid vibrations of the palm, breaking into sharp staccato a long-drawn, quavering yell. It is a signal of triumph, or victory and defiance, and is never used by the vanquished in either games or in war. Such was Coyote's "ruling" when the world was yet young, when the Animal People held sway.

81. McWhorter notes that this narrative was told by the Klickitat, Cascade, Wishom and Wasco tribes. Collected July 4, 1918; no informant is named.

82. In *Wishram Ethnography* Leslie Spier details the trade for horses, essentially at the main villages of the Wishram and Wasco, essentially with tribes from the East: Paiute, Nez Perce. See his "Trade," esp. pp. 225-228, wherein horses are frequently mentioned in trade. And see also "A Meeting with the Bannock and Paiute," esp. pp. 234-235 which avers the greatest interest of the Wishrams is in trading for horses.

83. For the origin of the horse among the Pima Indians, see the *Twenty-Sixth Annual Report of the Bureau of American Ethnology*, p. 241.

    That the horse was first brought to the New World by the gold-seeking Spaniard cannot be rationally gainsaid. The appellation "Cayuse," as now applied to the Indian pony of the Northwest, according to an intelligent and well-informed Walla Walla tribesman, came about in the following manner.

    During the war with Mexico, a band of the Cayuse Indians returning from a foray into Mexico brought with them some of the Mexican mustangs. These animals were referred to by the surrounding tribes as the "*Kuc-ci* [horse] of the Cayuse," or "Cayuse *Kuc-ci*." In time "Cayuse" became attached to all Indian horses of the *n-Che-wana*. One version of the story is that the fierce Cayuse were engaged to fight with the Americans in the Mexican War. The Bureau of American Ethnology is authority for saying that: "The horse, after the Indian had come into contact with the whites, was bred by the Cayuse, and from a merely local used word has extended currency in the Northwest Pacific states." (Alexander F. Chamberlain, in *Handbook of American Indians*, Part I, p. 225).

At best such attribution of the origin of the name must be regarded as highly hypothetical. The fact that the first appearance of the horse among various tribes of the Pacific states is buried in legend strongly attests that these people have been associated with their equine companion for a period covering many generations. It is indeed a long hark from Cortez's conquest of Mexico to the breeding of horses by the Cayuse in the wilds of the *n-Che-wana*.

84. Owl Child was, in his own right, an accomplished raconteur. And he dwelt at a place and time when Watlala Indians might have been met, their oral lore heard.

85. Some five years pass between the first telling of this narrative (See 9A above) and the present version. The outline of the narrative remains clear here, and is possibly enriched with further details from memory.

86. *Tos-cos wo-hah*: descriptive of an enormously long foot. While the narrator is a Wishom, the legend is that of the Cascades, a small tribe whose principal village was located at the Cascades of the *n-Che-wana*. The tribe has ceased to exist, having become absorbed among the more virile bands surrounding them.

87. Old Testament accounts of sons cuckolding their fathers include David by Absalom: II Samuel 16:22-23.

88. The Wishom name for Hood River (a stream as well as a town on the Oregon side of the Columbia River.)

89. "Big River," applied in general to the Columbia River, previously spelled "*n-Che-wana*."

SELECTED LIST OF READINGS FOR THE TENINO, UMATILLA, AND WATLALA OR CASCADES INDIAN NATIONS

A. GENERAL STUDIES

Attwell, J. 1974. *Columbia River Gorge history*. Skamania, Washington: Tahlkie Books.

Alvord, B. "Report Concerning the Indians in the Territories of Oregon and Washington." H.R. Exec. Doc. No.75 (Serial No. 906). 34th Congress, 3d Session, 1857. pp. 10-22.

__________, 1855. Concerning the Manners and Customs, the Superstitions, . . . of the Indians of Oregon. Vol. 5, *Information respecting the history, condition, and prospects of the Indian tribes of the United States*. ed. Henry Rowe Schoolcraft, 651-657. Philadelphia.

Cox, R. 1832. *Adventures on the Columbia River*, 2d ed. New York. 335 pp.

Culin, S. 1901. A summer trip among the Western Indians. *BFMUP*, 3:159-164.

Curtis, E. S. [1911] 1970. *The North American Indian*. See esp. volume 8, pp. 79-82. Reprint. New York: Johnson.

Eells, M. 1892. Aboriginal geographic names in the State of Washington. *American Anthropology* 5:27-35.

Gairdner, ---, 1841. Notes on the geography of the Columbia River. *JRGS* 11:250-257. [HRAF]

Kane, P. 1925. *Wanderings of an artist among the Indians of North America, from Canada to Vancouver's Island and Oregon*,. . . Toronto: The Radisson Society of Canada Ltd.. 329 pp.

Lee, D and Frost, J.H. 1844. *Ten years in Oregon*. New York: J. Collord. 344 pp.

Lockley, F. 1928. *History of the Columbia River Valley from the Dalles to the sea*. Chicago: S.J. Clarke. 3 vols.

McArthur, L. L. 1974. *Oregon geographic names*, 4th ed. Portland: Oregon Historical Society. 835 pp.

Meany, E.S. 1923. *Origin of Washington geographic names*. Seattle: University of Washington Press. 357 pp.

Meinig, D.W. 1968. *The great Columbia Plain: A historical geography, 1805-1910*. Seattle: University of Washington Press.

Moorhouse, L. 1906. *Souvenir album of noted Indian photographs*. Pendleton, Ore.: East Oregonian Print. 25 pp. with photos.

Newell, R. 1959. *Memoranda: travels in the territory of Missourie; travle to the Kayuse War; together with a report on the Indians south of the Columbia River*. Ed. by Dorothy O. Johansen. Portland, Ore.: Champoeg Press. 159 pp.

_____. 1984. *The People of Warm Springs: Profile: The Confederated Tribes of the Warm Springs Reservation of Oregon*. Warm Springs Reservation, Ore.: Confederated Tribes of the Warm Springs Reservation of Oregon. 80 pp.

Several calumnies refuted; or Executive Document No. 37. *Catholic World*. [February 1872]:665-682. [Ex. Doc. No. 37, U.S. Senate, 41st Cong., 3d Sess., 1870-71]. 18 pp.

Roe, F. G. 1955. *The Indian and the horse*. Norman: University of Oklahoma Press.

Schafer, J. ed., 1940. *Memoirs of Jeremiah Curtin* (Madison, Wisconsin.

Shane, R.M. 1957. "Warm Springs Indian Reservation" in *Jefferson County reminiscences, by many hands [copied by Helen Wing]*. Portland: Binfords & Mort. pp. 373-380.

Steeves, Mrs. S.H. 1927. *Book of remembrance(s) of Marion County, Oregon, pioneers 1840-1860*. Eugene.

Stewart, E. I., and J. R. Stewart, eds. 1957. *The Columbia River*. Norman: University of Oklahoma Press. [For original edition of Ross Cox, see above here].

Thwaites, R. G. ed. 1904-05. *Original journals of the Lewis and Clark Expedition*, 7 vols. New York.

Townsend, J.K. 1905. Narrative of a journey across the Rocky Mountains. *EWT* 21:349-351.

Vaughn, T. ed., 1971. *Paul Kane, The Columbia wanderer, 1846-47; sketches and paintings of the Indians and his lecture, "The Chinooks."* Portland: Oregon Historical Society. 154 pp.

Wallace, W.S. The intermontane corridor. *SWL* 18:38-46.

Wyeth, N. J. 1899. The correspondence and journals of Captain Nathaniel J. Wyeth, 1831-1836: a record of two expeditions for the occupation of the Oregon Country, with maps, introduction and index. . . ." In *Sources of the history of Oregon*, 1 [parts 3-4]. Edited by F. G. Young. Eugene: University Press.

B. RELIGION, SHAMANISM, MAGIC, THE MISSIONARIES

n. a., 1940. Feast of the salmon. *Oregon Historical Quarterly* 41:235.

Barnett, H. G. 1957. *Indian shakers; A messianic cult of the Pacific Northwest*. Carbondale: Southern Illinois University Press. 378 pp.

Boas, F. 1893. The Doctrine of souls and of disease among the Chinook Indians. *Journal of American Folklore*, 6:39-43.

Brouillet, J.B.A. 1869. *Authentic account of the murder of Dr. Whitman and other missionaries by the Cayuse Indians of Oregon in 1847*. Portland: S.J. McCormick. 108 pp.

Cocks, James F. III, 1975. The selfish savage: Protestant missionaries and Nez Perce and Cayuse Indians, 1835-1847. Ph.D. Diss., U. of Michigan. 245 pp./ Biblio. pp. 229-245.

Crowder, S. I. 1913. The Dreamers. *Overland Monthly* 62:607-609.

Drury, C. M. 1973. *Marcus and Narcissa Whitman and the opening of Old Oregon*. 2 vols. Glendale, Calif.: Arthur H. Clark Co.. Biblio. pp. 405-406.

_______. 1937. *Marcus Whitman, M.D., pioneer and martyr*. Caldwell, Id.: The Caxton Printers, Ltd.. 473 pp./Biblio. pp. 461-465.

DuBois, C., 1938. *The Feather Cult of the Middle Columbia*, 1-45. General Series in Anthropology, vol. 7. Menasha, Wis.: George Banta.

Gunther, E., 1926. An analysis of the First Salmon Ceremony. *American Anthropology*, n.s. 28:605-617.

_____, 1928. *A further analysis of the First Salmon Ceremony*, UWPA 2, No. 5, pp. 129-173. Seattle: University of Washington Press.

Harmon, R. 1971. Indian Shaker Church: The Dalles. *Oregon Historical Quarterly*. 72:148-158.

Huggins, E.L. 1891. Smohalla, the prophet of Priest Rapids. *Overland Monthly*, 17:208-215.

Jessett, T. E. 1973. *The Indian side of the Whitman Massacre*. Fairfield, Wash.: Ye Galleon Press. 53 pp./Biblio. pp. 51-53.

The last salmon feast of the Celilo Indians-Mid-Columbia. [Motion Picture] Portland: Oregon Historical Society, 1956. {18 min., sd., b&w, 16mm.}

MacMurray, J.W. 1887. The 'Dreamers' of the Columbia River Valley in Washington Territory. *Transactions of the Albany Institute* 11:241-248.

Park, W.Z. 1938. *Shamanism in Western North America*. Northwestern University Studies in the Social Sciences 2:1-166.

Randolph, J. 1957. Witness of Indian religion; present-day concepts of the Guardian Spirit. *Pacific Northwest Quarterly* 48:139-145.

Ruby, R. H. 1966. A healing service in the Shaker Church. *Oregon Historical Quarterly*. 67:347-355.

Smith, M.W. 1954. Shamanism in the Shaker religion of Northwest America. *Man* 54:119-122.

Spier, L., 1935. The Prophet Dance of the Northwest and its derivatives . . ., pp. 1-74. *General Series in Anthropology*, No. 1. Menasha, Wis., George Banta Publishing Co..

Stern, T., 1960. A Umatilla prophet cult. *ACISA* 5:346-350.

Strong, W. D., 1945. The occurrence and wider implications of a 'ghost cult' on the Columbia River, suggested by carvings in wood, bone and stone. *American Anthropologist* 47:244-261.

C. TRIBAL ECONOMIC STUDIES, CONTEMPORARY ACCOUNTS

Griswold, G. G. 1970. Aboriginal patterns of trade between the Columbia Basin and the Northern Plains. *Archaeology in Montana* 11:1-96.

_______, 1951. *The Indian dip net fishery at Celilo Falls on the Columbia River.* Bulletin No. 17, Oregon Fish Commission. Salem, Ore.

MacNab, G. 1972. A history of the McQuinn Strip, published November 22, 1972, *On the occasiion of the thanksgiving celebration commemorating return of the McQuinn Strip Lands to tribal ownership by the tribal council of the Confederated Tribes of the Warm Springs Indian Reservation.* Warm Springs, Oregon. 32 pp.

Michael, E. O. 1980. Governmental policies and the preservation and display of Native American cultural resources in the Middle Columbia Basin. Corvallis: M.A. Thesis, Oregon State University. 201 pp.

Shane, R.M. 1950. Early explorations through Warm Springs Reservation area. *Oregon Historical Quarterly* 49:273-309.

Toepel, K. A., et al. 1980. *Cultural resource overview of BLM lands in North-Central Oregon: archaeology, ethnography, history.* University of Oregon Anthropological Papers, No. 17. Eugene, Oregon. 215 pp.

U.S. Department of the Interior, Bureau of Indian Affairs 1957. Confederated Tribes of the Umatilla Indian Reservation: Constitution and Bylaws, Approved December 7, 1949. Washington, D.C.: U.S. Gov't Printing Office. 6 pp.

Warm Springs (Ore.) Indian Reservation Census Reports, 1886-1908. (National Archives Microfilm No. 595, roll 635). [Includes censuses for Paiute, Tenino, "John Day," Wasco tribes].

D. INDIAN TRIBAL HISTORY, WARS, REGIONAL RELATIONS

Brown, J. H. 1892. *Political history of Oregon. Provisional government, treaties, conventions, and diplomatic correspondence on the boundary question; . . . History of the Cayuse War. . .*, Vol. I. Portland: W.B. Allen. 462 pp.

Browne, J. R. Indian war in Oregon and Washington Territories. Special Report to the Secretary of War and the Secretary of the Interior, Dated December 4, 1857." 35th Cong., 1st Sess., House Exec. Doc. No. 38, pp. 1-66 (Serial set 955). Also in Sen. Exec. Doc. No. 40, Serial set 929, 1857.

Clark, R. C. 1935. Military history of Oregon, 1849-1859. *Oregon Historical Quarterly* 36:14-59.

Clemmer, J. W. 1980. The Confederated Tribes of Warm Springs, Oregon: nineteenth century Indian education history." Ph.D. Thesis, University of Utah. 260 pp.

Cliff, T. D. 1942. "A history of the Warm Springs Reservation, 1855-1900." M.S. Thesis, U. of Oregon. 323 pp./Biblio. pp. 273-284.

Curry, G. C. 1855. Expeditions against the Indians. In *Correspondence and Official Proceedings, Governor of Oregon Territory, George C. Curry, to the Citizens*. Salem, Ore.: Asahel Bush, Territorial Printer.

Deutsch, H. J. 1956. Indian and white in the Inland Empire: The conquest for the land, 1880-1912. *Pacific Northwest Quarterly* 47:44-51.

Doty, J. 1855. A True Copy of the Record of the Official Proceedings at the Council in the Walla Walla Valley, Held Jointly by Isaac L. Stevens Govn & Supt., W. T., and Joel Palmer, Supt. Indian Affairs, O.T. on the part of the United States with the Tribes of Indians Named in the Treaties Made at That Council June 9th and 11th, 1855. National Archives, Record Group 75. Washington, D.C.: Records of the Bureau of Indian Affairs. Available on Microcopy T-494, roll 5, item 3).

Glassley, R. H. 1972. *Indian wars of the Pacific Northwest*. Portland: Binfords and Mort. 258 pp.

_______, 1953. Pacific Northwest Indian wars. Portland: Binfords & Mort. 266 pp.

Gunther, E. 1950. The Indian background of Washington history. *Pacific Northwest Quarterly* 41:189-202.

Indian Hostilities in Oregon and Washington Territories. Message from the President of the United States, Transmitting the correspondence on the Subject of Indian Hostilities in Oregon and Washington Territories. U.S. 34th Congress. House 1st sess. Ex. Doc. No. 118, 1856. 58 pp.

Indian Hostilities in Oregon and Washington; Message from the President of the United States. U.S. 34th Congress, 1st sess., House Ex. Doc. No. 93, 1856. 144 pp.

Kennedy, J. B. 1977. The Umatilla Indian Reservation, 1855-1975; Factors contributing to a diminished land resource base. Ph.D. Thesis, Oregon State University.

Message from the President of the United States in Answer to a Resolution of the Senate, Calling for Further Information in Relation to the Formation of a State Government in California; and also, in Relation to the Condition of Civil Affairs in Oregon. U.S. 31st Cong., 1st sess., Senate Ex. Doc. No. 52.,1850. 180 pp.

n.a. 1972. *Memorial of the Legislative Assembly of Oregon Territory, August 10, 1848* (Fairfield, Wash.: Ye Galleon Press. 26 pp.

Parsons, W. 1902. *An illustrated history of Umatilla County, by Col. William Parsons, And of Morrow County, by W.S. Shiach; With a brief outline of the early history of the State of Oregon*. Spokane, Wash.: W.H. Lever. 581 pp.

Reese, J.W. 1965. OMV's Fort Henrietta: on winter duty, 1855-56. *Oregon Historical Quarterly* 66:132-160.

Ruby, R. H. and J. A. Brown 1972. *The Cayuse Indians; imperial tribesmen of Old Oregon*. Civilization of the American Indian Series, Vol. 120. Norman, Okla.: U. of Oklahoma Press. 345 pp./Biblio. pp. 313-330.

Stowell, C. D. 1987. *Faces of a reservation: A portrait of the Warm Springs Indian Reservation*. Portland: Oregon Historical Society Press. 197 pp/Biblio. pp. 190-192.

Thompson, E. N. 1964. *Whitman Mission: National historic site*. National Park Service Historical Handbook Series, No. 37. Washington D.C.: National Park Service. 92 pp.

Thompson, F. C. n.d. Interviews of Flora (Cushinway) Thompson, Wife of the late Tommy Thompson, chief of the Celilo Indians." n.p.. 3 tapes/ cassette [OHS].

Report of the Secretary of War. . . Relative to the Indian Disturbances in the Territories of Washington and Oregon. U.S. 34th Cong., 1st sess., Senate Ex. Doc. No. 66, 1894. 68 pp.

Victor, F. F. 1894. *The early Indian wars of Oregon*. Salem, Ore.: Frank C. Baker.

Whitman, Mrs. M. 1891. Letters written by Mrs. Whitman from Oregon to her relations in New York. *Transactions of the Oregon Pioneer Association* 19 [1891], pp. 79-179; 21[1893], pp. 53-219.

Whitman, N. P., 1986. *The letters of Narcissa Whitman*. Fairfield, Wash.: Ye Galleon Press. 245 pp.

F. FOLK ART, DECORATION, AND COSTUME

------, 1974. *Cornhusk bags of the Plateau Indians*, Cheney Cowles Memorial Museum, Spokane. Spokane: Eastern Washington State Historical Society. 12 pp.

Dreyfuss, S. 1983. A prism of carved rock; Dalles area rock art as an insight into Native American cultures. *Pacific Northwest Quarterly* 74:69-76.

Gogol, J.M. 1979. Columbia River Indian basketry. *American Indian Basketry Magazine* 1:4-9.

_______ 1980. Cornhusk bags and hats of the Columbia Plateau Indians. *American Indian Basketry Magazine* 1:4-11.

Haeberlin, H.K., H. H. Roberts and J.A. Teit 1928. *Coiled basketry in British Columbia and surrounding region*. 41st Annual Report, Bureau of American Ethnology. Washington, D.C., 119-484.

Kuneki, N. et al 1982. *The heritage of Klickitat basketry; A history and art preserved*. Portland, Ore.: Oregon Historical Society. 54 pp. / Biblio. pp. 53-54.

Ray, V. F., 1932. Pottery in the Middle Columbia. *American Anthropology*, n.s. 34:127-133.

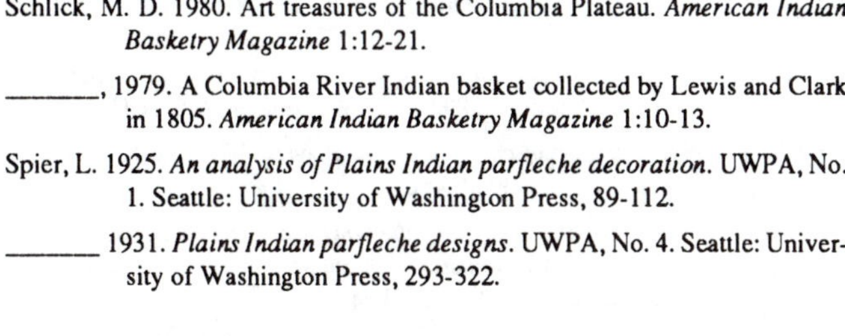

Schlick, M. D. 1980. Art treasures of the Columbia Plateau. *American Indian Basketry Magazine* 1:12-21.

_______, 1979. A Columbia River Indian basket collected by Lewis and Clark in 1805. *American Indian Basketry Magazine* 1:10-13.

Spier, L. 1925. *An analysis of Plains Indian parfleche decoration.* UWPA, No. 1. Seattle: University of Washington Press, 89-112.

_______ 1931. *Plains Indian parfleche designs.* UWPA, No. 4. Seattle: University of Washington Press, 293-322.

G. FOLKTALES, LEGENDS AND MYTHS

Clark, E. 1952. The Bridge of the Gods in fact and fancy. *Oregon Historical Quarterly* 53:29-38.

_______ 1953a. Indian story-telling of old in the Pacific Northwest. *Oregon Historical Quarterly* 54:91-101.

_______ 1953b. The mythology of the Indians in the Pacific Northwest. *Oregon Historical Quarterly* 54:163-189.

_______ 1955. George Gibbs' account of Indian mythology in Oregon and Washington Territories. *Oregon Historical Quarterly*, 56:293-325 [Part 1]; 57:125-167 [Part 2].

_______ 1953. *Indian Legends of the Pacific Northwest.* Berkeley: University of California Press.

Cornelison, J. M. 1911. *Weyekin stories: titwatit weyekishnim.* San Francisco: E.L. Mackey & Co.. 30 pp.

Hymes, D. H. 1953. Two Wasco motifs. *Journal of American Folklore* 66:69-70.

Lewis, N. M. 1909. Sunlight legend of the Warm Spring Indians. *Southern Workman* 38:685-686.

_______ 1910. The Warm Spring Indian legend of the fox and the spirits. *Southern Workman* 39:94-98.

Lyman, W. D. 1915. Indian myths of the northwest, *PAAS*, n.s. 25:375-395.

Ramsey, Jarold 1972. Three Warm Springs-Wasco stories. *Western Folklore* 3:116-119.

Randall, B. U. 1949. The cinderella theme in Northwest Coast folklore. *Columbia University Contributions to Anthropology*, 36:243-286.

Sapir, E. J. 1909. *Wishram texts, by Edward Sapir; Together with Wasco tales and myths, collected by Jeremiah Curtin. . .* Leyden: E.J. Brill, 1909. 314 pp.

Thompson, S. 1966. *Tales of the North American Indians.* Bloomington: Indiana University Press, 1966. See esp. "Sources," pp. 368 ff; also "Bibliography," pp. 373-386.

H. TRADITIONAL MUSIC, DANCE

Mooney, J. 1896. *The Ghost-Dance religion.* 14th Annual Report, Bureau of American Ethnology, 1892-1893. Washington, D.C., 641-1110.

Ray, V. F. 1937. The bluejay character in the Plateau Spirit Dance. *American Anthropology*, n.s. 39:593-601.

Spier, L. 1935. *The Prophet Dance of the Northwest and its derivatives: the source of the Ghost Dance*, in *General Series in Anthropology*, No. 1, 1-74. Menasha, Wis.: George Banta.

I. SOCIOLOGICAL, ANTHROPOLOGICAL, ARCHAEOLOGICAL STUDIES

Aikens, C. M. 1986. *Archaeology of Oregon.* 2d ed. Portland: U.S. Department of Interior, Bureau of Land Management, Oregon State Office. 133 pp./ Biblio. pp. 129-133.

Barry, J. N. 1927. The Indians of Oregon. *Oregon Historical Quarterly* 28:49-61.

Berreman, J. V. 1937. *Tribal distribution in Oregon*, in *MAAA*, No. 47:7-65. Menasha, Wis.: American Anthropological Association.

Biddle, H. J. 1926. Wishram. *Oregon Historical Quarterly* 27:113-130.

Boas, F. 1911. Chinook. Bureau of American Ethnology, Bulletin 40. Washington, D.C.. pp. 638-645, 650-654.

Browman, D. L. and D. A. Munsell 1969. Columbia Plateau pre-History: cultural development and impinging influences. *American Antiquity* 34:249-264.

Brunton, B. B. 1968. Ceremonial integration in the Plateau of Northwestern North America. *Northwest Anthropological Research Notes* 2:1-28.

Cook, S. F. 1955. The epidemic of 1830-1833 in California and Oregon. *University of California Publications in American Archaeology and Ethnology* 43:303-326.

Cressman, L. et al. 1960. *Cultural sequences at the Dalles Oregon; A contribution to Pacific Northwest prehistory.* Philadelphia: American Philosophical Society. 108pp.

________ 1937. Petroglyphs of Oregon. *UOSA* 2:1-78.

________ 1981. *The sandal and the cave; The Indians of Oregon.* Corvallis, Ore.: Oregon State U. Press. 81 pp.

Daugherty, R. D. 1956. *Early man in the Columbia Intermontane Province.* University of Utah Anthropological Papers, No. 24. Salt Lake City: University of Utah Press.

Dennis, E.F. 1930. Indian slavery in Pacific Northwest [3 parts] *Oregon Historical Quarterly* 31:69-81, 181-195, 285-296.

Driver, H. E. 1961. *Indians of North America.* Chicago: University of Chicago Press. 667 pp. / Biblio. pp. 613-633.

Elliott, T.C. 1934. Murder of *Peu-Peu-Mox-Mox. Oregon Historical Quarterly* 35:123-130.

Farrand, L. 1907. Des Chutes. Bureau of American Ethnology, Bulletin 30, Vol 1. Washington, D.C., 387-388.

______ 1907. Tyigh. Bureau of American Ethnology, Bulletin 30, Vol 2. Washington, D.C., 859-860.

______ 1907. Cayuse. Bureau of American Ethnology, Bulletin 30. Washington, D.C., 224-225.

French, D. 1961. The Wishram-Wasco. In *Perspectives in American Indian Culture Change*, ed. Edward H. Spicer. Chicago: University of Chicago Press, 340-430.

French, K. S. 1955. Culture segments and variation in contemporary social ceremonialism on the Warm Springs Reservation, Oregon. Ph.D. Diss., Columbia University.

French, K. and D. 1955. The Warm Springs Indian community," *AMI* 7:3-16.

Gibbs, G. 1967. *Indian tribes of Washington Territory.* Fairfield, Wash.: Ye Galleon Press. 56 pp.

Gunther, E. 1950. The westward movement of some Plains traits. *American Anthropology*, n.s. 52:174-180.

Hunt, H.F. 1918. Slavery among Indians of Northwest America. *Washington Historical Quarterly* 9:277-283.

Jacobs, M. A survey of Pacific Northwest anthropological research, 1920-1940. *Pacific Northwest Quarterly* 32:79-106.

Jorgensen, J. G. 1980. *Western Indians; comparative environments, languages and cultures of 172 Western American Indian tribes.*San Francisco: W.H. Freemason & Co.. 673 pp.

Krieger, H. W. 1927. Archeological investigations in the Columbia River Valley. *Smithsonian Institution Miscellaneous Collections* 38:187-200.

______ 1928. A prehistoric pit house village site on the Columbia River at Wahluke, Grant County, Washington. *Proceedings of the U.S. National Museum* 73:1-29.

Lewis, A. B. 1906. *Tribes of the Columbia Valley and the Coast of Washington and Oregon.* Memoirs, American Anthropological Association, Vol. I:147-209.

Mackey, H. 1972. New light on the Molalla Indians. *Oregon Historical Quarterly* 73:63-65.

Minto, J. 1900. The number and condition of the Native Race in Oregon. . . . *Oregon Historical Quarterly*, 1: 296-315.

Loring, J. M. and L. 1982-1983. *Pictographs and petroglyphs of the Oregon Country.* Los Angeles: Institute of Archaeology, University of California. 2 vols. Biblio., Vol 1:306-313; Vol 2:334-341.

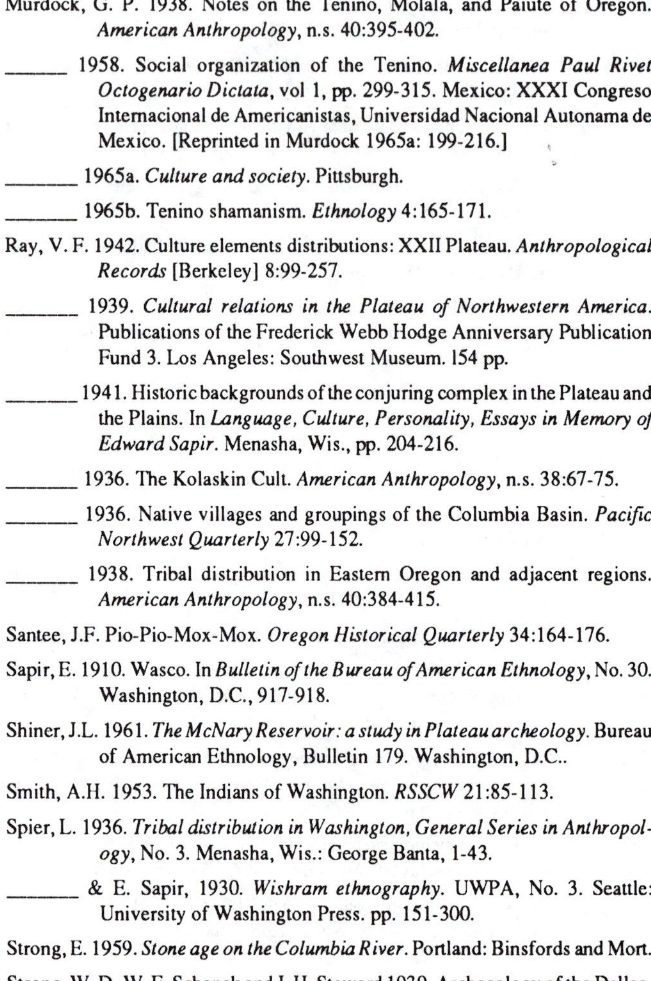

Murdock, G. P. 1938. Notes on the Tenino, Molala, and Paiute of Oregon. *American Anthropology*, n.s. 40:395-402.

______ 1958. Social organization of the Tenino. *Miscellanea Paul Rivet Octogenario Dictata*, vol 1, pp. 299-315. Mexico: XXXI Congreso Internacional de Americanistas, Universidad Nacional Autonama de Mexico. [Reprinted in Murdock 1965a: 199-216.]

_______ 1965a. *Culture and society*. Pittsburgh.

_______ 1965b. Tenino shamanism. *Ethnology* 4:165-171.

Ray, V. F. 1942. Culture elements distributions: XXII Plateau. *Anthropological Records* [Berkeley] 8:99-257.

_______ 1939. *Cultural relations in the Plateau of Northwestern America*. Publications of the Frederick Webb Hodge Anniversary Publication Fund 3. Los Angeles: Southwest Museum. 154 pp.

_______ 1941. Historic backgrounds of the conjuring complex in the Plateau and the Plains. In *Language, Culture, Personality, Essays in Memory of Edward Sapir*. Menasha, Wis., pp. 204-216.

_______ 1936. The Kolaskin Cult. *American Anthropology*, n.s. 38:67-75.

_______ 1936. Native villages and groupings of the Columbia Basin. *Pacific Northwest Quarterly* 27:99-152.

_______ 1938. Tribal distribution in Eastern Oregon and adjacent regions. *American Anthropology*, n.s. 40:384-415.

Santee, J.F. Pio-Pio-Mox-Mox. *Oregon Historical Quarterly* 34:164-176.

Sapir, E. 1910. Wasco. In *Bulletin of the Bureau of American Ethnology*, No. 30. Washington, D.C., 917-918.

Shiner, J.L. 1961. *The McNary Reservoir: a study in Plateau archeology*. Bureau of American Ethnology, Bulletin 179. Washington, D.C..

Smith, A.H. 1953. The Indians of Washington. *RSSCW* 21:85-113.

Spier, L. 1936. *Tribal distribution in Washington, General Series in Anthropology*, No. 3. Menasha, Wis.: George Banta, 1-43.

_______ & E. Sapir, 1930. *Wishram ethnography*. UWPA, No. 3. Seattle: University of Washington Press. pp. 151-300.

Strong, E. 1959. *Stone age on the Columbia River*. Portland: Binsfords and Mort.

Strong, W. D., W. E. Schenck and J. H. Steward 1930. Archaeology of the Dalles-Deschutes region, *UCP* 39:1-154.

Strong, W. D. and W.E Schenck 1925. Petroglyphs near the dalles of the Columbia River, *American Anthropology*, n.s. 27:76-90.

Sturtevant, W. C. ed. 1978. *Handbook of North American Indians*. Washington, D.C.: Smithsonian Institution. See esp. Vol. 7.

Suphan, R. J. 1974. *Oregon Indians II: ethnological report on the Wasco and Tenino Indians; ethnological report on the Umatilla, Walla Walla, and Cayuse Indians: commission findings*. American Indian Ethnohistory Series: Indians of the Northwest. New York: Garland Publishing Co.. 534 pp.

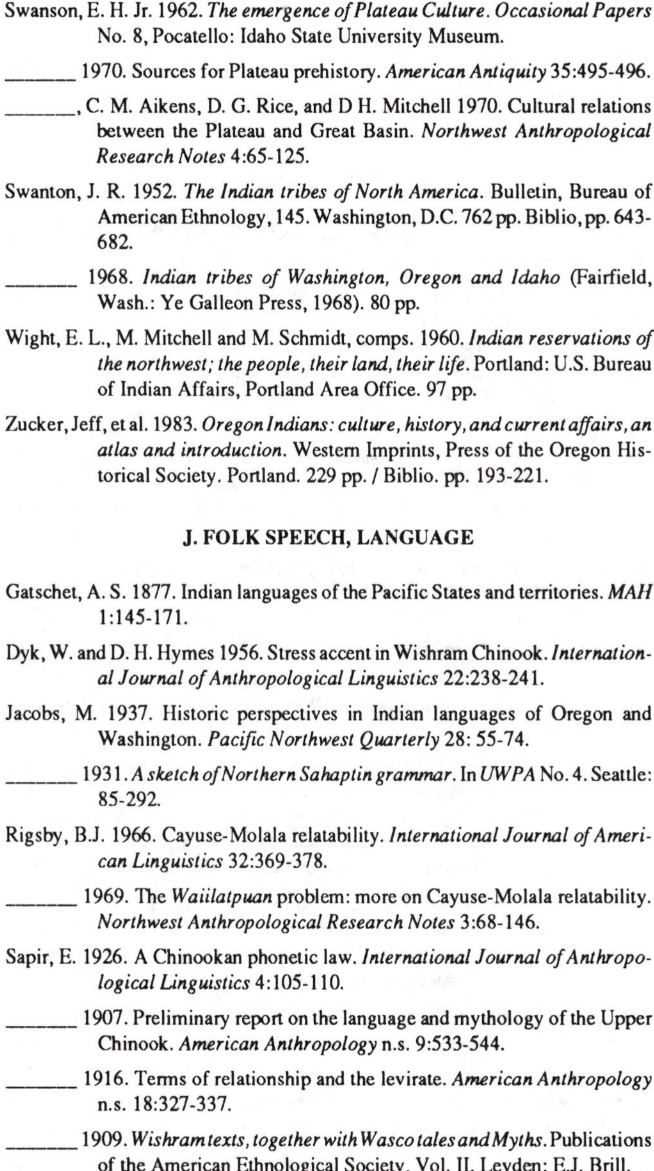

Swanson, E. H. Jr. 1962. *The emergence of Plateau Culture. Occasional Papers* No. 8, Pocatello: Idaho State University Museum.

_______ 1970. Sources for Plateau prehistory. *American Antiquity* 35:495-496.

_______, C. M. Aikens, D. G. Rice, and D H. Mitchell 1970. Cultural relations between the Plateau and Great Basin. *Northwest Anthropological Research Notes* 4:65-125.

Swanton, J. R. 1952. *The Indian tribes of North America*. Bulletin, Bureau of American Ethnology, 145. Washington, D.C. 762 pp. Biblio, pp. 643-682.

_______ 1968. *Indian tribes of Washington, Oregon and Idaho* (Fairfield, Wash.: Ye Galleon Press, 1968). 80 pp.

Wight, E. L., M. Mitchell and M. Schmidt, comps. 1960. *Indian reservations of the northwest; the people, their land, their life*. Portland: U.S. Bureau of Indian Affairs, Portland Area Office. 97 pp.

Zucker, Jeff, et al. 1983. *Oregon Indians: culture, history, and current affairs, an atlas and introduction*. Western Imprints, Press of the Oregon Historical Society. Portland. 229 pp. / Biblio. pp. 193-221.

J. FOLK SPEECH, LANGUAGE

Gatschet, A. S. 1877. Indian languages of the Pacific States and territories. *MAH* 1:145-171.

Dyk, W. and D. H. Hymes 1956. Stress accent in Wishram Chinook. *International Journal of Anthropological Linguistics* 22:238-241.

Jacobs, M. 1937. Historic perspectives in Indian languages of Oregon and Washington. *Pacific Northwest Quarterly* 28: 55-74.

_______ 1931. *A sketch of Northern Sahaptin grammar*. In *UWPA* No. 4. Seattle: 85-292.

Rigsby, B.J. 1966. Cayuse-Molala relatability. *International Journal of American Linguistics* 32:369-378.

_______ 1969. The *Waiilatpuan* problem: more on Cayuse-Molala relatability. *Northwest Anthropological Research Notes* 3:68-146.

Sapir, E. 1926. A Chinookan phonetic law. *International Journal of Anthropological Linguistics* 4:105-110.

_______ 1907. Preliminary report on the language and mythology of the Upper Chinook. *American Anthropology* n.s. 9:533-544.

_______ 1916. Terms of relationship and the levirate. *American Anthropology* n.s. 18:327-337.

_______ 1909. *Wishram texts, together with Wasco tales and Myths*. Publications of the American Ethnological Society, Vol. II. Leyden: E.J. Brill.

K. GAMES

Butler, B. R. 1958. The prehistory of the dice game in the Southern Plateau. *TEBIWA* 2:65-71.

L. BIBLIOGRAPHIES

Ault, N. A. 1959. *The papers of Lucullus Virgil McWhorter.* Pullman: Friends of the Library, State College of Washington. 144 pp.

Bonnerjea, B. comp. 1963. *Index to bulletins 1-100 of the bureau of American ethnology; with index to contributions to North American ethnology, introductions, and miscellaneous publications.* U.S. Bureau of American Ethnology, Bulletin 178. Washington, D.C.: U.S. Gov't Printing Office. 726 pp.

Bjoring, B. and S. Cunningham, 1982. *Explorers' and travellers' journals documenting early contacts with Native Americans in the Pacific Northwest, 1741-1900*, Bibliographic Series, University of Washington Libraries, No. 3. Seattle: University of Washington Libraries. 15 pp.

Butler, R. L. comp. 1937. *A check list of manuscripts in the Edward E. Ayer Collection, The Newberry Library.* Chicago: The Newberry Library. 295 pp.

Carriker, R. C. and E. R. 1987. *Guide to the microfilm edition of the Pacific Northwest Tribes missions collection of the Oregon Province Archives of the Society of Jesus.* Wilmington, Del: Scholarly Resources. 97 pp.

Field, T. W. 1873 [1951]. *An essay towards an Indian bibliography. being a catalogue of books, relating to the history, antiquities, languages, customs, religion, wars, literature, and origin of the American Indians, in the library of Thomas W. Field.* New York: Scribner, Armstrong, and Co.. [Repr. Long's College Book Co., Columbus, Ohio]. 430 pp.

Freeman, J. F. comp. 1966. *A guide to manuscripts relating to the American Indian in the library of the American Philosophical Society.* Memoirs of the American Philosophical Society, vol. 65. Philadelphia: American Philosophical Society. 491 pp. {But see "Kendall" below}.

_______ 1970. *Index to literature on the American Indian.* Published for the American Indian Historical Society. San Francisco: Indian Historian Press, 1970).

Hewlett, Leroy comp. 1969. *Indians of Oregon; A bibliography of materials in the Oregon State Library.* Salem. 125 pp.

Kendall, D. comp. 1982. *A guide to manuscripts relating to the American Indian in the library of the American Philosophical Society.* Memoirs of the American Philosophical Society, vol. 65s [supplemental]. Philadelphia: American Philosophical Society. 168 pp. {See "Freeman" above}.

Larner, J. W. comp. 1987. *Guide to the scholarly resources, microfilm edition, of the papers of the Society of American Indians.* Wilmington, Del., Scholarly Resources. 74 pp.

Murdock, G. P. and T. J. O'Leary. 1975. *Ethnographic bibliography of North America*, 4th ed.. New Haven: Human Relations Area Files Press. 5 vols.

Schuster, H. H. 1982. *The Yakimas, a critical bibliography.* Bloomington: Indiana University Press. 158 pp.

Seaburg, W. R. 1982. *Guide to Pacific Northwest Native American materials in the Meville Jacobs Collection and in other archival collections in the University of Washington Libraries.* Communications in Librarianship, No. 2. Seattle: University of Washington Libraries. 113 pp.

Young, F. G. ed. 1897-1899. *Sources of the history of Oregon.* Eugene: University Press.

ACKNOWLEDGEMENTS

A. I am grateful to the the staff of the Special Collections Division, University of Washington Libraries, for permission to publish the following photographs:

Edward S. Curtis photos: #10, #137, #138, #140, #142, #144, #149, #150, #163, #179, #181, #201, #202, #205, #221.

Frank LaRoche photo: #638

Major Lee Moorhouse photos: #593, #1491

Joseph Dixon photo: #4021

Still other photos appear which were taken by the author during August 1988 using a Nikon F3 with a Nikkor 28 mm. wideangle lens and Kodak Tri-X film.

B. I am grateful to the editors of *Ethnology* for permission to publish the map of Tenino trails, Villages and Camp Sites herein.

C. Cover design by Hannah Ueno,
Unamics Inc., NW 115 State St., Suite 213, Pullman, WA 99163

D. Desktop publishing by Karen Savage,
The Computer Workshop, 1311 NE Ravenna Blvd., Seattle, WA 98105

ORDER FORM

Great Eagle Publishing Inc.
3020 Issaquah-Pine Lake Rd. SE
Suite 481
Issaquah, WAshington 97801-7255
FAX (206) 391-7812

Please send ____ copies of THE FORGOTTEN TRIBES at $10.95 per copy. I understand that I may return any books for a full refund — for any reason, no questions asked.

name ____

address ____

city ____________________________ State _____ zip __________

phone ____

SALES TAX

Please add 8.2% for books shipped to Washington addresses.

SHIPPING

Book Rate: $1.75 for the first book and $0.75 for each additional book (Surface shipping may take three to four weeks)

Payment: ____ **Check**

___ Credit Card: ___ Visa ___ MasterCard ___ AMEX

___Other ____________________________

Card number: ____________________________

Name on card: ____________________________

Expiration date:_____/_____